W9-ABG-366

Alice in Wonderland

DALE H. GRAMLEY LIBRARY
SALEM COLLEGE
WINSTON-SALEM, N. C.

MERLIN HOUSE

DISTRIBUTED BY E. P. DUTTON, INC.

Alice in Wonderland

THE FORMING
OF A COMPANY AND THE MAKING
OF A PLAY

PN
2297
N28
M3
1973

Copyright © 1973 by Rabbit Hole, Inc.

———————————

All rights reserved. No part of this publication
may be reproduced or transmitted in any form or by any means,
electronic or mechanical, including photocopy,
recording, or any information and retrieval system now known or to
be invented, without permission in writing from the publishers,
except by a reviewer who wishes to quote brief
passages in connection with a review written for inclusion
in a magazine, newspaper, or broadcast.
Published simultaneously in Canada by Clarke, Irwin & Company
Limited, Toronto and Vancouver.
Distributed in the United States by E. P. Dutton, Inc.,
201 Park Avenue South, New York, N.Y. 10003

Library of Congress Catalogue Card Number: 72-98394
ISBN 0-88306-001-9 (Clothbound)   ISBN 0-88306-002-7 (Paperback)

Caution: This play in its printed form is designed
for the reading public only. All dramatic rights in it are fully protected
by copyright, and no public or private performance, professional
or amateur, may be given without the written permission of the author
and the payment of royalty. As the courts have ruled that
the public reading of a play constitutes a public performance, no such reading
may be given except under the conditions stated above. All
communications should be addressed to the author's representatives.
For all professional rights: Audrey Wood, International
Famous Agency, Inc., 1301 Avenue of the Americas, New York, N.Y. 10019.
For all amateur rights: Dramatists Play Service, Inc.,
440 Park Avenue South, New York, N.Y. 10016

———————————

First Printing
Manufactured in the United States of America

THE PLAY

CREATED, PERFORMED AND WRITTEN BY
THE MANHATTAN PROJECT

GERRY BAMMAN
TOM COSTELLO
SASKIA NOORDHOEK HEGT
JERRY MAYER
ANGELA PIETROPINTO
LARRY PINE

UNDER THE DIRECTION OF

ANDRE GREGORY

ACKNOWLEDGEMENTS

Lyn Austin, Kenneth Cavander, National Endowment for the Arts,
New York State Council for the Arts, Billy Rose Foundation, New York University
School of the Arts, Rockefeller Foundation, Jeannette Seaver, Phil Haber,
Leigh Porter, Soho Studio, Robert Bishop, Gideon Lewin, Peter Waldman, Jeff Niki
Lee Spiegelman, Ken Wood, Jim MacDonald

THE BOOK

DESIGNED BY

RUTH ANSEL

TEXT BY

DOON ARBUS

PHOTOGRAPHS BY

RICHARD AVEDON

CONTENTS

THE TEXT

edited by Doon Arbus from a series
of taped conversations with each of the seven members
of the Manhattan Project, recorded between
January 11 and September 4, 1971. It is a collective account
of the forming of the company, the way *Alice in Wonderland*
was chosen, and how it was made into a play.

THE PHOTOGRAPHS

taken by Richard Avedon
in his studio in a series of twelve sittings between
November 1970 and April 1971,
interpreting moments from the finished production. They
are divided into the following scenes:

THE PLAY

created by Gerry Bamman, Tom Costello, Andre Gregory,
Saskia Noordhoek Hegt, Jerry Mayer, Angela Pietropinto, and
Larry Pine, based on Lewis Carroll's *Alice in Wonderland*
and *Through the Looking Glass*. It was developed
during two years of rehearsals at the New York University School
of the Arts and in performances at Brecht West, New
Brunswick, New Jersey, Syracuse University, The Loft Theater
in New York City, and Harvard University's Loeb
Drama Center. The play opened in New York at the Extension on
October 5, 1970, and has subsequently been performed
at the Holland, Spoleto, Shiraz, Berlin, Paris,
and Edinburgh Festivals, and at the Performing Garage in New York.

THE PLASTIQUES

details of an exercise originally developed
by Jerzy Grotowski and the Polish Laboratory Theater,
and freely interpreted by the Manhattan Project
as part of the actor's training.

Gerry Bamman

Andre Gregory:
director

John Holms:
stage manager

Franne Lee:
costume designer

Eugene Lee:
set designer

Angela Pietropinto

Tom Costello

Jerry Mayer

Saskia Noordhoek Heg

Larry Pine

Gerry: **I**n the spring of 1968, Andre was scheduled
to come to NYU . . . where all of us except Saskia were enrolled . . . to
direct a six week project. His reputation had preceded him.
He had just directed *Leda Had a Little Swan* on Broadway,
which had closed before it opened. Before that, he had been
fired from a production in Los Angeles. And six months earlier
he had been fired from Philadelphia. We didn't know what
to expect. We'd been warned about not letting him take advantage
of us; remarks like, "All of us have our quirks, but Andre
Gregory has a few more than most so if he gets his kicks from
watching you beat one another up, don't go too far."

Angela: He was supposed to be this young, infamous,
crazy director.

Gerry: So he walked in. My initial response to new directors is
always to turn my back on them and wait and see
whether I can trust them or not. As if all my talent was in
my breast. To this day Andre still says that the most
sinister aspect of that first meeting was this guy who went over
in the corner and kept looking at him over his shoulder.

Angela: To me he looked like anything but a mad genius.
He was very tan and he had on this sort of Cardin suit,
like the Playboy of the Western World.

Larry: He was wearing this 1940's suit with pleated pants . . . much too
big for him . . . and a narrow tie. And he had suspenders.
I saw him and I thought, Jesus Christ!

ANDRE
GREGORY

Alice in Wonderland

A
BOOK
ABOUT
A
PLAY

THE
JABBERWOCKY

" 'Twas brillig and the
slithy toves did gyre and gimble
in the wabe; all mimsy were
the borogroves and the mome
raths outgrabe . . ."

DOWN
THE RABBIT
HOLE

"when suddenly a white
rabbit with pink eyes ran right
by her. In another moment,
down went Alice after it."

THE FALL

"down, down, down . . .
would the fall never come to
an end? I wonder if I shall fall
right through the Earth . . ."

The forming
of a company and the
making of a play

Jerry: Larry and Tom and I had jobs at Lincoln Center during the six weeks of Andre's class, so the three of us weren't involved in that. We were up at Lincoln Center making money carrying spears. It was so horrible that we'd wander down to the school from time to time and watch the work Andre was doing with the class.

Larry: One day I went over to see what they were doing. I got there late, and instead of going in I peeked through the keyhole. All I could see was that Gerry Bamman had hold of this girl by the tits; he had her crotch to crotch and was making these weird noises, bouncing up and down. I could see Andre's face, too; he was grinning and squirming around in his chair, watching it all. I was overcome with relief that I wasn't in on this one.

Gerry: Toward the end of the six-week project at NYU, Andre mentioned something about forming a company. I still don't know whether it was just a cavalier remark or really serious. But we jumped at it. And we kept expanding the vision of what this company would be.

Jerry: The idea really touched a chord in us. I had seen what they were doing in that workshop, and it was fantastically funny. People were rolling in the aisles. So as soon as I heard that Andre had mentioned something about forming a company, I went up to him and said, "If you're really going to do this thing I want to be in on it, too." He said, "Sure."

Gerry: Jerry Mayer was turned on just by watching the rehearsals, so he didn't need any convincing. Tom and Larry weren't sure, but they trusted Angela and me and felt it would be great if we could all stay together. It meant they had to give up other jobs in order to do it. We all did: we'd all signed letters of agreement or contracts with regional theaters.

Tommy: One day Andre invited us all to have some wine at a restaurant and talk about forming a company. I liked the people so I said, "Sure, great." Andre had never met me before and he kept looking at me out of the corner of his eye. I could see he was wondering how the hell he was going to fit me into this thing.

Larry: I don't know why I said yes, especially after what I'd seen through the keyhole. There was something about him, though. His eyes. Just something. I said, "Okay." I had nothing to lose.

Angela: It was a gamble for all of us. But Andre has the kind of charisma that makes you take a crazy gamble. As far as I was concerned there wasn't even a question of choice. I had to try it, give it a chance.

Larry: I didn't know Andre at all, but I had a lot of faith in him. I don't know why. I had no reason to. But somehow I knew we were all going to work together and we were going to do something very special.

Gerry: We knew he was talented. We knew he was a good director. We could tell from the workshop. But we still didn't know what kind of a man he was personally. If you're entering into a long-term relationship with somebody, that does matter. I looked upon it as a love affair. Not a marriage. So if it ran out, I was all set to heigh-ho down the road. And if it lasted, great.

Andre: Talking about any of the actors individually, at least at the beginning, is very hard. Grotowski once said that there's no such thing as talent, only lack of talent. So, in the beginning, the actors for me were like clay. Just as I was like clay.

Larry: I think Andre could have taken any group of halfway intelligent people and done the same thing. Just happened it was us.

Gerry: When we separated for the summer it looked as though we were going to have nothing. NYU had refused to give us any rehearsal space. We had no money. All we had was this idea that we were a company.

By the time we met again in September, we had gotten NYU to let us have a room to work in at night. And Andre had worked out an agreement with the Rockefeller Foundation to have $7,000 funneled to us through the school. So things looked a little more hopeful. But Andre still said that it would be a miracle if we managed to stay together.

Andre: We all needed to hide from a theater system where you have three weeks to rehearse. Where you can't be really honest with each other because when a play closes you may never see each other again. Where you always work toward a specific, decided goal before you begin, rather than discovering the goals out of the rehearsal process itself.

We didn't know what our goal was. We were never sure whether we'd finish a work. To go into a little room for two years, never knowing if you will accomplish anything, is lunacy. But it was vital for us.

9

Gerry: I think anybody in the theater who can go to the circus and not be impressed by an acrobat doing a triple somersault off a trapeze into somebody's arms is crazy. Not only because of the physical demands involved; just by the sight of two people trusting each other that way. It's a peculiar kind of trust. It comes from two bodies responding to each other and knowing — those bodies knowing — that they are safe in each other's hands. Anything that can help conquer that instinctive physical distrust is important to actors. Maybe to everyone, but certainly to actors.

Andre: The actors had gone through a period of circus training at NYU and I think it was very valuable to our work. They had learned to juggle, to somersault. But there was one essential circus lesson they hadn't absorbed: the acrobat's gut sense of timing. He has to know exactly how long each of his turns can last. If his timing is off by a split-second it can kill him. I think that's a vital lesson for people in the theater, not so much because of the physical dangers, although they do exist, but because I believe each moment in the theater has a limited life span. If it's drawn out too long it starts to wilt.

Gerry: Achieving that kind of physical trust in one another is more complicated than the ability to do any particular exercise. But doing nothing will never get you there.

Andre: As long as you act only with the words or with the eyes, there's a place where you're safe. But if you release the body, if you can find a way in which the body must commit itself, then you enter a very unsafe area in which anything may be said.

Saskia: A few months before Andre came to NYU, Grotowski taught a workshop there. It was only supposed to be for people in the school, but I knew Grotowski's work and decided I just had to get into that class. I sat outside in the hall until finally he said I could join. That's where I met everybody. But when the class ended, I didn't see any of them again for a long time.

Larry: We had all worked with Grotowski at NYU and we showed Andre all the exercises we thought we knew, such as walking like a porpoise, with your arms and shoulders rotating in opposite directions.

Andre: I wanted an actor who could fly. Physically fly.

Saskia: When I first came to this country from Holland I was a sack of potatoes. I didn't have any sense of my body. I was walking with my pelvis tipped back, and I didn't even know it. I walked very stiff, like a soldier. It was all involuntary. I still walk that way but now I can control it.
    Working with Grotowski was the first time I found out anything about the body. I bruised my toe the first week because I couldn't get up on my head, and I was angry about that. I wanted the result instead of feeling out the spine. After I had worked with Grotowski, I became very interested in the body. I wanted to know everything. I wanted to see skeletons, see the shoulder blades, the spine, the pelvis, how it all fits together.

Andre: Grotowski developed the Exercise Plastique based on Meyerholdt's Biomechanics and the Kathakali Theater in India. It divides the body into about forty set gestures from head to foot, involving all parts of the body. Each movement in the series of gestures has about three separate parts. The actor starts with his first impulse, say a detail of the head, a circular motion of the head on the neck. He commits himself to that gesture until the impulse begins to run out, then frames or freezes, like a stop action film. Then he goes to the next gesture his impulse suggests.

The exercise may inspire a physical association. For example, one of the trademarks of the Plastiques is a certain hand gesture. In the process of that movement, the actor might begin to feel that he was playing a game of handball. That association would make him commit his entire body in a sport way. At another time, though, the same gesture might make him feel as though he was running his hand through molasses. That would result in a more sensual commitment throughout the rest of the body.

After about half an hour of this exercise, the actor is completely wiped out.

DALE H. GRAMLEY LIBRARY
SALEM COLLEGE
WINSTON-SALEM, N. C.

Larry: We went through Grotowski's recipe book, *Towards a Poor Theater,* and were doing all the exercises, not just the Plastiques but these other things, too. We'd been doing them for months I guess, very religiously, but we hadn't experienced any magical transformations.

Gerry: They were some of the most pain-giving, body-racking, torturing exercises that I have ever been through. In one of them, you have to walk around the room holding your ankles. Then you walk around the room for a while holding your toes. There was another where you walk as though your arms and legs are on strings, like a puppet. Later we found out that Grotowski had given most of these up.

Andre: We also gave them up, because Grotowski pointed out that not only had he given them up but that one of them—the one to do with the knees—if done for too long, could leave you a cripple for life. But we continued with the Plastiques.

Jerry: For about a year and a half—a long, long time—I felt that those exercises were just calisthenics. That all this mystical shit about them was just that: mystical shit. But something does happen with Plastiques that is impossible to explain—at least I can't—and only makes sense when you find it out for yourself. It took me about a year and a half to learn that. Most of the time it was just calisthenics.

I would always argue that we shouldn't waste our time doing that crap. God damn it, let's put a play together, open it and see what happens. I had no patience at all.

But that's my deficiency, not the Plastiques'. I don't see the mystical side of things very easily.

Tommy: Those exercises were great for my body, but they weren't always as fulfilling as people said they would be. They could be drudgery. And whenever that happened, I would say to Gerry Bamman, "Would you please share your dream with me again. Just explain to me what this is all about." Gerry always seemed to have some way to keep it all going for himself.

Andre: When I worked with Strasberg, if an actress was shy about committing her breasts, he would say to her, "You're shy about committing your breasts." The actress would then have to ask herself why, and probably the only way she could answer that question would be to spend a few years on the analyst's couch.

The wonderful thing about the Plastiques is that you never ask why. You just commit the breasts, you commit the head, commit the groin, commit the shoulders. If no association comes up, that's all right, but you have committed that area of the body and slowly you're breaking down physical masks.

Some actors in the group have found the Plastiques more valuable than others. They can be used for purely physical reasons, to explore what your body can do beyond the ways in which you're accustomed to use it. But that effect seems limited to me. I think its greatest value is in opening up the imagination through physical commitment.

Jerry: Once I discovered what Andre and Gerry Bamman, who had always been very much into the physical side of the work, were talking about, it became easier to do the exercises. The hardest part is deciding to do them. Because you can do them mechanically. But then nothing happens. So you have to decide to *really* do them. Decide to hurt. Once you get into that they do carry you through. And then all the things they say about them are more or less true. The mind does jump and the body goes right with it. But I must admit the Plastiques are still not my favorite form of recreation.

Andre: I think there's a great misconception about improvisation. It is often understood as self-indulgent. Play without purpose. I think what it really means is what the painter does. If he has a problem drawing a certain hand, he will draw a hundred sketches of that hand until he feels his way into the one he wants. In the Plastiques the actor is improvising, but he is doing it within a very strict physical vocabulary. There are specific gestures, a wide variety of them, but very precise. It is a true discipline. And it helps to teach one of the central tasks of performance—that in order for there to be freedom there must be discipline. The words, the physical gestures never change. Those external details are like the highway with its own signposts, and you must follow them. Your freedom lies in the spirit in which you travel that road.

Larry: We were also trying to work on a play called *'Tis a Pity She's a Whore*. We were having some problems with it, seeing as how it's a fifty-character play and there were only six of us.

It was at that point that Andre decided to go and study with Grotowski for a while. While he was gone we continued to meet and tried to work. Most of the time, though, we just sat around and stared at one another for hours.

Andre: I really think it's important that a director go through the acting process and personally experience whatever he asks his actors to do.

Gerry: I went to France with Andre to study with Grotowski. That period must have been hardest for the people who remained behind in New York. They didn't have anyone there to keep them going. Every night during the three weeks I was in Paris I went home and made a tape recording to send back to the others so they wouldn't feel totally abandoned.

Andre: Grotowski has a theory that there are different vocal resonators throughout the body, that one can speak not only from the mouth or the throat, but from the chest, the back, the top of the head. And he does a lot of work in trying to open up those vocal resonators.

In one of those exercises, to get at the resonator in the top of the head, you walk around the room saying, "Hello, ceiling. Hello, ceiling." Trying to throw your voice out of the top of your head at the ceiling, trying to wipe the ceiling with your voice. I could see it was working for some people but I kept doing the Hello, Ceiling bit, I really tried, and it got me nowhere.

Finally Grotowski said to me, "Try to find in yourself an animal who would live in its head. Where the head is the center of its life." At first I started going for the most obvious turn-on animals like lions and bears, but suddenly I got the idea of a giraffe.

I started walking around the room, very erect, committing my neck, which seemed like the center of a giraffe's life. I felt my neck getting longer and longer. And I began to see that all sorts of jungle trees were below my neck and I could bend my head and pluck the fruit; I was walking through the jungle, getting prouder and prouder of this incredible neck and head. Suddenly Grotowski said, "Sing," and my voice was like a penis raping up through the center of

my head and a sound came out of me that was like Ima Sumac. I was thinking, "Son of a bitch, what am I doing?"

Then I heard Grotowski say, "Feel the glass table." There was a glass table at the other end of the room and the glass was vibrating from this sound.

Gerry: There never was a glass table in that room.

Andre: It's very grueling physical work Grotowski puts you through. He makes you do exercises that break down blocks in your body, and it's terrifying, both physically and emotionally. I think everyone who works with him reaches a point where they get terribly depressed, and it becomes a question of whether they have the courage to break through the wall. I was miserable, and I kept wondering what the hell I was doing there in France, in leotards, standing on my head for this guy who was only two years older than me.

I had hardly spoken to Grotowski at all during the first few weeks. I was very intimidated. One night he asked me to have dinner with him. He wanted me to help him translate a letter. He was nursing a cold, so we drank a lot of *vin chaud,* which is red wine and cognac, really powerful stuff. We talked for hours about everything but the theater and finally parted at about four o'clock in the morning. I went back to my hotel, fell asleep, and had this dream:

I was walking with Grotowski and the eight
other actors in a kind of Garden of Eden. It was
shady and cool and there were trout jumping in
the brook and deer leaping. Grotowski and I were
having a fascinating discussion about Nietzsche and
Plato—which is interesting, because I don't know a
thing about either of them—but the discussion was
fascinating. One by one the others in the group
began to disappear until only Grotowski and I
were left. He said to me, "I am going into the
burning desert. It will be terrifying, but you may
come if you want." I said, "Sure, I'd like to." We
started toward the burning desert, but somehow I
lost him. I found myself in a dreary city of
skyscrapers. Grotowski was gone, and suddenly
I was up on the thirteenth floor of one of the
buildings and there was no ledge around the
balcony. I was clutching my work script and one
of my legs was caught in a bicycle wheel. As I
was trying to free my leg, the work script dropped,
and I was on the verge of plunging after it
when the window opened and there stood Joseph
and the Virgin Mary. Joseph said to me, "If you'll
make love to Mary, we'll give you sanctuary." I
said, "Sure." And I did. But of course, as it must
be with the Virgin Mother, it was a special kind
of love-making. Sort of sexual and not sexual.
After this act of love Joseph took a hypodermic
needle and gently injected a bubble of air into
Mary's arm and in complete peace she died. I then
found myself back in a room with Grotowski. He
gave me my work script, and then he put on my
head and shoulders the furs of the Princes of all
the Russias like out of an Eisenstein movie. And
with my work script under my arm and the furs
on my head and shoulders, with my body growing
strong and proud, hand in hand Grotowski and I
walked into the burning desert.

I awoke from this dream filled with the most
incredible peace. Shortly after I returned to the
group to work, we chose *Alice*.

Larry: When Andre got back from France he said he'd
          had a spiritual rebirth. He'd had a vision and now
          we were going to find the right piece of material.
          We all said, "Oh, good!" And we waited.

Gerry: We got back from France around the middle of
          December and got very little work done that
          month. I doubt if we rehearsed with Andre more
          than four days.

—————————

Tommy: I don't remember how we decided on *Alice*. I must have been out of the room. I think I'm always out of the room when the important decisions are made. I was probably in the john.

Angela: Andre kept asking us to read plays. I hate reading plays and I wouldn't. But at the time I happened to be reading *Alice in Wonderland*. We had a meeting, where Andre and the others were talking about plays I'd never heard of, because I'm so ill-read.

Gerry: We were all sitting around in a little circle, and Andre was asking questions. We'd talked about all kinds of plays. None of them rang a sympathetic vibration. So he began asking, "If you had your choice, what role would you like to do most? What piece of literature? What theater? What director?"

Andre: One person wanted to work at the Guthrie, one at the Royal Shakespeare, one with Grotowski. One wanted to play Hamlet; another, Lady Macbeth. When it came to film directors, four said Fellini.

Larry: I don't remember what everybody answered. I don't even remember what I answered. I think there was a moment of silence. So I said, to get the conversation going again, "I just saw a good movie. I just saw *Yellow Submarine*." And somebody said, "Yeah, let's do *Yellow Submarine*." And I said, "We can't. It's been done."

Jerry: The idea of *Alice in Wonderland* came from Angela.

Gerry: She piped up in this tiny voice and said, *"Alice in Wonderland."* And then she giggled.

Angela: I turned to the person next to me and mentioned *Alice in Wonderland*. Whoever it was said, "Oh, yeah. Let's do *The Wizard of Oz*." I said, "No!"— by that time I was talking at the top of my lungs— "The whole point is that *Alice in Wonderland* really isn't a child's story."

Andre: There was a moment of silence.

Larry: We all looked at each other. We'd all read *Alice* at some point in our lives.

Jerry: Everybody said, "Hmmm, there's something to that."

Angela: Andre said, *"Alice in Wonderland*. That's a terrific idea!"

Andre: We just knew it was right.

Larry: Andre said, "Let's get a copy of it."

Gerry: We all went out and bought it and read it that same night.

Larry: We saw all those animals and all those crazy people and we knew it was right. It had endless possibilities.

Angela: We started reading some of the play versions, the one by Eva le Gallienne and others, but they all seemed saccharine sweet. So we went right to the book.

Gerry: Andre said, "Read it and tell me which characters turn you on."

Jerry: I don't remember what I wanted to be. I think I may have had a thing for the Mad Hatter. But I didn't know the book at all, and I'm slow about developing a feeling for a character.

Gerry: We all had a list of characters we liked. Where the choice was easy and didn't conflict with anyone else's, you got it right away. There were no arguments about suitability. Except for Angela. Angela didn't want to play Alice.

Angela: When we were choosing roles, Andre told us to write down what we wanted to be. I wrote the Dormouse and the White Queen. I knew I didn't want to be Alice. I found her a drag. In the book she came across to me as very staid, almost prudish. She's always trying to fit things into what she's been taught. She seemed like a stiff little English girl, and I had no cerebral or visceral contact with her. She was everything I hated.

Andre: Angela is convinced I conned her into playing Alice. I'm not at all sure it wasn't she who was doing the conning. After all, Alice is the role of a lifetime. She was being incredibly cunning. She had to be, to suggest *Alice in Wonderland,* get the role, and leave all of us feeling she was some kind of martyred good sport for playing it.

Angela: Andre took me out for coffee and, in his usual way, was not telling me I had to be Alice but was explaining to me how wonderful the character of Alice was, so that I'd want to do it. And I said, "The only thing that really saves this girl is the fact that it's all her dream." And Andre said, "Exactly. Exactly. I see it that this is her dream, the audiences' dream, they're Alice, I'm Alice. We're all Alice."

ALICE AND LEWIS

"I am going to make you the biggest thing in the biggest parade in the biggest city in the world . . . THE BALLOON PRINCESS!"

THE LITTLE DOOR

"We've got to make that door bigger."

DEFLATING THE BALLOON PRINCESS

"I don't want to be bigger than you. I don't want to be the Balloon Princess . . . I was bad. Look I'll punish myself. See . . . sssssssss . . ."

Larry: We started out trying to do that scene where Alice gets larger and smaller. We had Angela out there and we kept saying, "Okay Angela, you've got to really act this thing. You've got to make us believe that you're getting bigger and you're getting smaller and that there are these doors all around you." And poor Angela was out there grunting and struggling and trying to convince us.

Tommy: One day somebody said, "Lewis Carroll can tell the story." I got all excited and said, "Oh, I want to play Lewis Carroll. Let me play the dirty old man." I had a picture in my head of a lecherous Walter Brennan or something.

Larry: Andre wasn't there that day. We'd all been pressuring Angela until finally Tommy said, "Wait a minute. I've got an idea. I'm just going to talk you through it, Angela. My name is Lewis Carroll. I'm your friend. I'm going to tell you this story and I want you to play as if it's really happening to you." So he started telling the story, and Angela started responding to it.

I thought it looked terrific. Right away, as soon as Tommy mentioned Lewis Carroll, I thought, "Oh boy, dirty old man–little girl scene." I saw the whole scene as a dirty old man trying to feel up this little girl in different ways by telling her a story. So I was sitting there, watching and rooting for Tommy. I don't think the idea appealed to Angela too much.

Andre: At first we went through a period of dealing very specifically with Tommy as Lewis Carroll, a man obsessed with little girls and unable to communicate directly with people. For a while he was working with a stutter because Carroll stuttered. But most of that work turned out to be a dead end. Tommy isn't Lewis Carroll.

Tommy: I think the best way an actor can work is out of himself—adopting characteristics of other people along the way, but basically using himself.

ENTERING THE POOL OF TEARS

"Ssssssssea serpent.
Salt sea. Sea of tears . . .
your tears."

Andre: There is only one stuttering moment left in that scene. Alice is trying to guess the opposite of eating and she asks for a clue. Lewis tries to give her one and gets stuck on the "d" in drinking.

Tommy: Lewis does a lot of mean things to her in the scene. Won't let her get through the door. Makes her get tiny. Makes her huge. Forces her into the water. I kept falling into the trap of being very aggressive with her. Really ugly. Because I was doing so many mean things to her. It was Andre's idea that all Lewis really wants is to get Alice to play it his way. He's miffed at her, but never aggressively cruel.

Angela: Tommy can manipulate people. He loves to control things. With women, he can't help it really, he's a little condescending. Calls them little angels. And I know he's doing it and I think he knows I know.

Tommy: We worked a lot trying to find out about my need to control this scene. The scene is about control.

Angela: When it goes well, it's like two friends, maneuvering to see who will come out on top.

Gerry: What Angela and Tommy came up with is completely their own. Most of the dialogue came out of improvisations. And physically, it's entirely free-form.

Angela: The scene was so much ours. For me it really was the key to *Alice*. And still is. If I try to do anything, if I don't fly with my impulses, it becomes cute. Insipid. A big girl playing a little girl.

Tommy: It was the first scene we worked on, and it literally took a year to do. By the time we had finished, it had in a way set the style for the whole play.
   We went through hours and days and days and months of rehearsals. Every day we did a completely different improvisation. I tried stuffing Angela into sausage skins. Blowing her up like a balloon. Anything to get her bigger and smaller and through the doors. We tried real doors. We tried other actors as doors. We tried pantomiming doors. And each day Andre would pick out some tiny piece here and there and say, "Let's keep that."

Angela: I find myself doing things as Alice that I wouldn't even do at parties. Making ugly noises. Sitting with my legs apart. I'm totally unself-conscious. There's one moment in that scene when Alice is little and is trying to get the key. She runs at Lewis and climbs up him, straddling him with her legs. I remember when that first happened in rehearsal, Tommy made a remark about it afterward. And I suddenly thought, "My God, look at the way I was wrapped around a man!" But that was a thought about Angela and Tommy. When it happened in the improvisation it was totally impulsive. It came right out of Alice trying in any way she could to get what she wanted.

Tommy: I knew I had to make her get big. Somehow I had to. One day, in one of the improvisations it just happened. Lewis says to Alice, "I'm going to make you the biggest thing in the biggest parade in the biggest city in the world." She says, "The balloon!" And he blows her up.

Then one night at a party I met some agent Andre knows. He grabbed me by the lapels and started shaking me, saying, "Thirteen hundred dollars a week! I got this kid a job for thirteen hundred dollars a week! I can make you a star!" This guy just stuck in my head.

All of a sudden during rehearsal one day, when Alice said, "The balloon," I turned into that agent at the party. I'd been thinking about him, and it just came out. I said, "The balloon? I spit on the balloon. It's the Balloon Princess!" Because I knew that guy wouldn't have anything as lowly as a mere balloon. It really tickled me that I had gotten to something I felt was true about that guy. And we kept it.

Andre: There's one wonderful moment in which Alice throws herself into Lewis' arms for sympathy. He's about to hug her but he can't. Not fully. His inability to hug her leads to a frustration with himself and an anger at her. It's out of that impulse that he creates the Dirigible Prince, which is a very cruel and very funny moment. I really feel that at that point there's a connection between Carroll's inability to express himself and Tommy's. I think they come together there.

Tommy: In everything you do you realize that the idea has been there long before you come out with it. That it's been sitting around in the back of your mind or worked out intellectually. Something. But it's been there. It has a history.

See, I'm a junk collector. I guess you can say that's my hobby. I find things on the street and I bring them home with me—pieces of wood, glass doorknobs, strips of metal—real junk. And they lie around my house driving my wife crazy. But then one day I'll make something out of them. It'll all come together and I'll make something. That's the way Andre works. I love that.

Andre: When I was a child I had a doll named Bridget. The strange thing was that I was more of a mother to Bridget than a father. Something terrible happened to her. I got scarlet fever and Bridget was contaminated so they took her away and burned her. The day I came down with scarlet fever I was watching the Macy's Thanksgiving Day Parade from the third floor of the Hotel Pierre on Fifth Avenue, where we were staying, and floating by, above my head, came this huge dirigible man.

Tommy: The Dirigible Prince is my favorite moment in the play. I'm sure that's my own creation. It came out of a very frustrating period when I was trying to get Angela to go along with what I was doing, and she kept saying, "Well, that doesn't work because I'm not really *impelled* to go through the door." It was driving me out of my mind. So finally I got got my revenge; I made this evil balloon. It was such a triumph. I knew I loved it. But of course it's Andre's eyes that say so.

Angela: The whole scene with Tommy came out of a truth in our relationship. He's manipulating me. Or trying to. I guess because I'm a woman. I really think that in the relationship between Alice Liddell and Lewis Carroll she knew exactly what she was doing. When you read the diaries, it's just amazing. Or if you see some of those pictures he took of her. Wow! She knew exactly what she was doing to this man. As Angela I know that I can use my femininity on Tommy to get things I want from him. If I'm weak and need help, he loves being the man and controlling the situation.

Andre: There are very few moments in the production that I'm sure were my ideas. When they come I really love them. One is in the Alice and Lewis scene when they mirror each other and then he turns her into a marionette and her voice gets very low and his very high. One day, in rehearsal, I said to them, "Let's see what would happen if you mirrored each other." Something really assertive like that.

Tommy: For that whole mirror bit I did a lot of improvisations to get at the feminine things in me. I played at being different women I knew.

Andre: Tommy's very bright, and he always knows when I'm not happy with something. For a long time I was unhappy with his first scene. I couldn't say why. I think I was waiting for him to really become a man, for some sort of physical transformation in him.

I remember the day it happened. I had him do an improvisation in which he became his mother and went to a dress shop to find a dress. It was horrible to watch and probably very difficult for him to do. But I think the fact that he was able to be a woman also made him able to be a man in the scene. It all changed for me after that.

Tommy: It was amazing the difference in movement I got to. And it had nothing to do with anything homosexual. As I remember it, the thing that did it for me was actually looking for a dress. Really shopping.

Andre: The entire scene is filled with sexual ambiguity. The change in identities and roles. Who's the man and who's the woman? In a funny way those questions of role reversal are part of the theatrical process. Who is who? Is it the actor? Is it the role? How do you tell the difference? At its best, a performance becomes a kind of labyrinth of those questions.

_____

Larry: Shortly after we chose *Alice* and were so excited, all of us juiced up to the hilt ready to work, Andre split. That's the way Andre works. He gets people all juiced up and ready and then he splits. He doesn't like people to work when they're overexcited.

Angela: He always does that. He gets you excited and then he goes away.

Larry: He went up to Yale to do *The Bacchi*—which turned out to be a bomb.

Gerry: So we'd lost him again. Or we thought we had. The longer he was gone, the more our suspicions grew. At one point we were so paranoid that we'd go through Andre's briefcase whenever he left the room to see if he had any new contracts. We started feeling that his frequent absences were a roundabout way of telling us he was disenchanted with the whole idea and didn't want to be there. We would have periodic meetings about who we would get to replace him. We must have been insane. All of us. Just off in another world. If you start a company like ours you can't bring in somebody new to replace the director. That's thinking in Broadway terms, for Christ's sake.

Angela: We used to have little get-togethers about it at my house. My big argument always was that, even if the man was Satan himself, the company was something he wanted. As long as he wanted it, and we wanted it, it was all right.

Gerry: Andre was a terribly difficult person to get to know and to respond to. He had been through a year of hell: three failures that were at least in part of his own making—which he himself admitted. He was always telling wild, impossible stories, which was very unnerving for people who were uncertain whether or not to trust him. Often, we'd meet for a rehearsal, and after an hour he'd suddenly have to leave. It got so bad at one point that we started making bets about whether or not he'd show up. It began to panic us.

Larry: When Andre left for Yale he said, "You all just keep working on *Alice in Wonderland* while I'm gone." Every day we'd gather together and read it. We read it and reread it.

Gerry: We tried to keep going, but it was so hard without somebody there, some authority figure to say, "Okay, let's begin."

Larry: I can't do scenes. I mean, I can't go off with another actor and work on a scene. I just hate it.
When Andre's there he'll say, "What do you want to work on?" And you'll say, "I want to work on the fact that my hemorrhoids hurt." And he says, "Good. Great. You work on that." Then he'll run over to the other person and he'll say, "What do you want to work on?" And the other person will say, "I want to work on the fact that my mother died ten years ago." So you have two actors coming together, one working on his hemorrhoids and the other working on his dead mother, and neither knows what the other is doing. And Andre just sits there and watches.
But when he's not there, both people are acting, but at the same time, both are playing Andre's part, watching. Only now there are two different Andres and they keep getting in each other's way.

Gerry: Poor Andre. When he got back from Yale, after about six weeks, he walked into a viper's nest. I think he was totally bewildered by the mistrust he found, although he should have sensed what was happening. But he walked in and all fucking hell broke loose.

Larry: I didn't have any scenes. Everybody had done scenes except me, so I was feeling guilty. Bad. When Andre got back I said, "I'm sorry, Andre, I don't have any scene work. I just can't do scenes." He said, "Yeah, I know just what you mean." I have no idea whether he really did, but everything turned out okay. I got the parts I wanted.

Gerry: Tom started calling Andre the worst possible names. Said he was a masochist. Beating himself into the ground. Firing himself from theaters. And now he was taking us along with him. Andre got called everything from a dilettante to a traitor.

Tommy: There were times when I thought we'd never put it all together. We'd been working for a year, and people kept saying from time to time that we ought to put on a production. One day Andre came in and said, "I just hired this brilliant designer." About a month later he said, "This great designer has shown me these great designs he's going to do for us." Building up my hopes. One day he walked in in the middle of a frustrating rehearsal and said, "I fired the designer today." And I went crackers, man. I said, "We're never going to put this together. You are self-destructive and . . ." I just went crackers.

Andre: I had always felt that Tommy wanted—and needed—my admiration. I was waiting for him to stand on his own. He had always been very sweet with me, always trying to make sure I was okay. Maybe to make sure I would treat him the same way. So when Tommy started lashing out at me, I was stunned. It wasn't surprising from other people in the group but it was totally against the style of Tommy's behavior with me. I think it took a lot of courage. Of course, I was very hurt. Probably because there was an element of truth in what he said.

Gerry: The one miracle to me is that Andre never quit. There must have been times when he thought, My God, what am I doing with this bunch of meshuginers? I can go direct some place else. I know he was tempted. And he could have. But he never did.

_____

Gerry: Getting into Alice was very difficult. I suppose that's true of anything: beginnings are hard. We did a lot of outside reading. A lot of research on Carroll. It became clear that many of the characters in the book were based on people in Carroll's life and in Alice Liddell's life. So we decided to try and build the whole thing around Alice's family.

Andre: Saskia came into the group late, around the time of the family improvisations. She had been trying to see me about joining the group and I vaguely knew what she looked like — like an eccentric aunt out of an Agatha Christie novel — so it seemed absurd.

Saskia: When Andre gave his workshop at NYU I had gone to find out if I could work with him. I felt very ill at ease meeting him. His eyes troubled me. They were very piercing. And I felt shy. Andre told me that I should go work with another director who does a lot of physical work. I guess he didn't want me there at that time.

Angela: I remember the first time I met Saskia, before she even joined the group. I thought she was from somewhere behind the Iron Curtain. I saw her as a crazy, fanatical librarian, always in browns and somber colors.

Saskia: Around the middle of April I wrote to Joe Chaikin of the Open Theater asking if there was a possibility for me to work with him. He invited me to come to one of their rehearsals. I had seen the company's work and liked it a lot. So I went to a rehearsal. That same evening Chaikin called and told me it would be impossible for me to join. There were too many girls in the group already and besides, he said, I needed more physical work. I wept and wept.

Andre: Angela had told me that Chaikin was interested in Saskia. I figured if that was true, there must be something there.

Saskia: About two weeks later Andre called and wanted to have lunch with me. It was at Ratner's. I'll never forget. Andre started by saying that he thought I would make a good member of the company. But in the meantime I had seen his *Bacchi* up at Yale and I didn't like it. So instead of answering him I started asking him questions. "Why do you want this company?" And he began explaining how he had had several big shows before but they seemed very hollow to him. He wanted to start from the beginning and relax into the simplicity of things. It was funny, because I was really interviewing him. I was still nervous, but asking all those questions made me feel good. It was a nice talk. I joined in May. They had just started rehearsing *Alice.*

Andre: By now it was summer. We were doing our craziest work. Or what seemed the craziest. I was trying to find the beginning of the play. I had read the annotated *Alice,* in which there are constant references to who the characters in the book are in Alice Liddell's life. So, to see if it might get us anywhere, we started going through a whole series of family improvisations in which Alice wanted impossible things like being a racing driver or going to join her boyfriend in Vietnam. Real soap opera.

During this same period, we would have these spooks — sometimes spirits from her past and sometimes parts of her — who kept trying to force their way into her to make her go into Wonderland and set them free. And they couldn't use words, just sounds. The result was some very interesting vocal work, but we didn't realize it was vocal work until months later.

We'd been together for almost a year and suddenly we found ourselves in this crazy summer with the Liddells and the spooks. People began losing their minds.

Gerry: Andre was committed to experiment. Not to experimental theater—which is an old concept—but to work itself. To work without knowing where it might lead. To just keep working until something resulted and then see what it was.

Angela: I really felt all along that Andre knew what he was doing. Sometimes I got depressed because it was taking so long, but even then, I believed that it was because Andre knew how much time we needed to become a company.

Larry: So these family improvisations started. Angela was Alice. Saskia was her sister. Gerry Bamman was their father.

Andre: A lot of it was to give Gerry Bamman the experience of being a father.

Larry: Gerry had always assumed a role of authority in the group. Next to Andre, he was the one who really saw that things got done, took care of the business end of things, directed the exercises. We'd all looked on Gerry as a kind of leader.

Gerry: Jerry Mayer kept saying that he didn't feel like part of the family and Andre would ask him, "What do you feel like? If you feel like an outsider, you can be an outsider in the improvisations. Maybe you feel like a grandfather who isn't included."

Larry: So Jerry Mayer, who always has a hard time finding where he's at, became a rich grandfather. Tom was Lewis Carroll, a friend of the family. And I was a weird uncle from New York.

Saskia: Andre was trying to build an ensemble, so he thought it would be a good idea to see everything in terms of this family. The rest of the group seemed to be in a down period. But I had just begun, and I felt I had joined the ideal group. It

was just what I had always wanted. No bullshit with people at the top imposing things on you, making you a puppet. It all seemed full of roses.

Larry: Different things kept happening within this family. One time Alice is running away from home. Or Alice gets pregnant. Alice sleeps with her father. Or Alice has died. She's been in a plane crash and we're all at the airport waiting for her plane to land. How are we going to act around each other now that we've lost Alice? I was playing the weird uncle from New York, and one day I decided I wanted everyone to take off their clothes. So I said, "Hey, I've got a good idea. Why don't we all take off our clothes." Everybody looked at me. Just looked at me. Except for Tom Costello, who immediately took off all his clothes. I really hadn't expected anybody to do it. Not that taking off your clothes is such a big thing. I just hadn't expected that anybody would ever do anything I suggested.

Jerry: Those family improvisations were sheer hell. The worst period I've ever spent. I was having serious doubts about the whole thing.

Gerry: There was no money. Our seven thousand dollars ran out pretty quickly. All the men were driving cabs at night. Sometimes Andre would come in with a thousand-dollar check he'd raised from someone. After *The Bacchi,* he had started teaching at Yale once a week and often he'd just turn that money right over to us. But it was a very despairing time.

Jerry: A lot of allegiances, alliances, and friendships had been formed while we were at NYU before Andre ever came along. But Saskia was new to the group. And she's a pushy broad. She had pushed her way into the Grotowski seminar, pushed her way into NYU, and now she was pushing her way into the group. So we were having a hard time getting along. All her strengths seemed like selfishness to me.

Larry: Saskia's crazy. Was crazy from the beginning. She's a totally impulsive person. Nothing rational about anything she does. One of her first days she came in and started this improvisation, walking around the room, spouting, "Blech ghuh yech kchaw." Really disgusting. It turned Andre on.

Jerry: Another day she did an improvisation that I thought was a piece of dreck from beginning to end. Andre liked it, though, and so did everybody else.
My problem was, I had to figure out some way to get along with her. Because what it came down to was that I couldn't trust her. And couldn't work with her. So the two of us had a long talk. It didn't solve the whole problem between us. But it was a start.

Gerry: Jerry Mayer refused to let himself get involved in the family improvisations. He thought they were useless. So he'd stand off to one side and watch. Many improvisations were set up to deal specifically with his sense of isolation.

Andre: I think each person, at one point or another, wanted to quit. Had a real passionate desire to leave.

Gerry: Except Angela. She was the one person who was absolutely unfailing in her belief and her desire to stick with it.

Angela: That period wasn't really that bad for me. I always seem to feel that whatever is happening is for the best. When I was teaching in the high school system—Chelsea Vocational High School for Boys—and getting zapped in the halls and everything, it was a horrible period in my life. But at the time it didn't seem so bad.

Gerry: There were times when we worked only with sounds. The first scene in *Alice* takes place by a stream. She and her sister are reading a book. It's a quiet summer day.
We tried to create the water and the quiet summer afternoon with spirits, movement, sounds. Some of the most abstract, impossible work developed out of that. I don't mean that it was irrelevant. It may well have been a stage we had to go through to reach a point where we were willing to use just sounds or movement to convey something. Perhaps the forest in the production now could never have happened without our first trying to be a water spirit. But at the time it seemed totally chaotic.

Andre: We were like six people in the middle of a huge clock trying to figure our way out of the machinery.

Tommy: We did things, man, you wouldn't believe. In the opening, with the rowing, we thought it might be nice if the entire company played water sprites. We're all lying on the floor being water sprites, making all these liquid motions and gurgling sounds. We very quickly decided that this wasn't leading anywhere, but we continued to pursue it. And some of the sounds that were in that water sprite period are in the opening. The shhh's and the tic tocs. So nothing is ever lost.

Gerry: I think I was the first one to try to quit. I had really had it. I was sure that I could never do this kind of work. Andre had been saying all along that the theater we all knew was naturalistic and he didn't necessarily want to do something naturalistic. It might end up that way, but he wanted to feel free to try anything. I would always argue with him, because naturalism was all I knew. The schools don't teach anything else. So the more we got into things like being a bloop-bloop water sound, or being a dream figure and trying to act out your dreams, the more lost I became. And this was all piled on top of my distrust of Andre.

So I came in one day that summer and said I was going to quit. I had nowhere else to go, but I just felt I had to admit I couldn't cut this and go do something that I could. So I spoke to Andre, who said, "Let's all talk about it." We talked for hours about it. Saskia said she thought I shouldn't quit, that I should see a psychiatrist. Saskia's never been one to mince words. Everybody said his piece.

Except Larry. Larry didn't say anything.

Larry: Everybody was talking, you know. It's just that I can never think of anything to say.

Gerry: He looked out the window. He had a stick in his hand and kept hitting it against things, but he didn't say anything. This went on for hours. And finally Larry made his speech.

Larry: Finally I said, tears welling up in my eyes—it was like doing a bad scene—I said, "Listen, man, you can't leave. I mean you *can* leave but not as far as I'm concerned. Because if you leave, I'll hate you. I'll never forgive you. We need you."

Gerry: He started by saying, "Well, God damn it, I'm not going to let you quit. I don't allow you that right. You can walk out if you want to. You can go. But as far as I'm concerned, you're not quitting. I'm not going to let you. I'm not going to say, 'Go ahead, fuck you.' *You're* the one that talked me into this because you needed it so badly. *You're* the one that had to have this company. And *you're* the one who organized it all and talked everybody into doing it and promised everybody the world, and now you come in here and you tell us you're not good enough for this work. Oh, bullshit!"

Larry: That was the one and only time I've ever said anything like that to anybody. And it was the truth when I said it. Looking back it seems kind of schmaltzy, but at the time I meant it. I did need him. He was kind of a barometer for me. All my life I've looked up to somebody—not someone that I idolize but someone I trust. And as long as that person is hanging in there, so am I.

Gerry: It was one of the funniest things I've ever heard. There I was in a state of moral crisis, and I was laughing so hard the tears were rolling down my face. He was launching into this thing against me that was so brutal, and at the same time so funny, that the incongruity kept knocking me from side to side. He said, "You're always walking out on people. You've done it with girls. With dogs. But you're not doing it to me. I mean you say you lost your dog while you were walking it. Well, I'm suspicious of that, too!" One of the greatest crises in my life was losing my dog and here he was telling me I'd walked out on her.

Larry: I knew that someday Bamman was going to be a dynamite actor. I said, "Someday, Gerry, you're going to be a very, very good actor, and I want to be around when that happens." So he said, "Okay. I'll stay." And he stayed.

Gerry: By the time Larry was finished the whole mood had changed from an earnest, tear-ridden discussion into a whole comedy. And he was right. It would have been impossible for me to quit after that. Impossible.

That was the first of a whole series of such things. There would be days when we would spend hours talking somebody out of this kind of mood. I was the first.

Larry: Tom was going crazy, too, at one point. He'd come in all hunched over, with his nose and mouth covered in his coat, I suppose because he didn't want to say anything. And he'd mumble, "I'm going crazy, Andre, I can't stand it." And Andre would talk to him.

Angela: Tommy would get disgusted every once in a while. But I think that he wanted the same thing Andre wanted, so it was all right if he was being used.

Tommy: I'd put too much into this already. I'm the kind of person who clings to what he has. I'd put a year of work in there, man. I wasn't about to let that go.

Jerry: I think it was right in the middle of the family improvisations with the Liddells that I seriously contemplated giving it up. I couldn't fit into the improvisations with the other people. It became an insurmountable obstacle for me. I think what was really going on during that period was that we were building an ensemble. But I didn't realize that at the time. I don't think anyone did.

Larry: Finally Jerry came in and said: "I guess I just don't understand the way you work, Andre." So we all went through the same thing with him.

Gerry: We pleaded. We cajoled. No means was too devious or low for us. The only thing we never employed was physical force. But we used every sort of moral bludgeon possible.

Once I had been through it, I discovered a great rationale for myself which I used on everyone else: having put this much in, you had to see it through. Just out of curiosity you've got to stay.

Larry: Andre wasn't saying a word. You can always tell when Andre's got something on his mind. He picks and chews at his fingers, and his sense of humor is totally out the window when he's upset. Finally he said, "If anybody tells me one more time that he wants to leave, it's over. Finished. I'm leaving." When Jerry heard that, he said, "I guess in that case I can't leave because I wouldn't want to fuck the rest of the people up."

Jerry: By then it would have been very difficult for anyone to leave the group. Whenever I'd get depressed and convince myself that this whole thing would never happen I'd think back to the workshop project that Andre did and ask myself: "Was it really that good?" "Yes." "Was it really that funny?" "Yes." And I'd look at the parts of *Alice* that worked. Tommy and Angela's scene has always made me fall out. I think that is the funniest goddamn thing I've ever seen. And each time I watched it, it gave me new hope.

Larry: The next week—the very next week after Andre had threatened to quit—Angela came in and said she had to leave: her husband had gotten a job in Chicago. At that time I was going through one of my hate-Angela phases, and I thought, "Oh, good! Angela's going to leave. Now we can get some work done."

We went through two hours with her. I had to leave and go out in the hall and giggle. I was crazy. I was literally loony, and I would go out in the hall, stifle my laughter, get control of myself, go back in and listen to everybody talking, and then run out in the hall and giggle some more.

Angela: The family improvisations had been going on forever, and Andre felt that the rest of the group was not really facing the fact that Alice wants to get away from her family when she goes into Wonderland. So after rehearsal one day he came to me and said, "I want you to tell the group that you have to leave because your husband has gotten an important commission in Chicago and the two of you are going out there to live." I didn't want to do it. But Andre kept insisting that the group needed to face up to what it would be to lose me, to lose Alice. And finally he convinced me.

I thought about it all night. I began to feel very guilty about it, sneaking in the back door to their emotions instead of trusting their acting ability. And on top of that I was sure they'd never believe me because I'm a terrible liar. The next day I explained to Andre how I felt about it, and he told me to leave the room for a while and he'd prepare everybody, tell them that I was upset about something. When I returned, I started to speak but burst into tears. I kept crying and telling them I had to leave, and I saw that they really believed me. Fortunately Andre didn't keep it going too long.

Larry: Finally Andre told us it was all a joke. That he just wanted to see how we'd react, since this was in the improvisation period that Alice was running away from home. I went up to Andre and said, "Listen, I was happy when Angela said she was going to leave." And he said, "That's good. That's good. Use that. Use that." Well, that's where a lot of the work is at.

Gerry: Angela had an incredible, unflagging energy. No matter how often she was thrown around, battered down, knocked about or how many times she's gone through a scene, if Andre said, "Let's do it again," she'd bounce up like a little rubber ball. And keep bouncing.

Larry: One Christmas before *Alice* opened in New Jersey, I went out to Mexico to visit some friends of mine on a commune. I'm from that part of the country, but I'd forgotten how beautiful it was: the spaces, the sunsets, the mountains. And my friends seemed so happy. I wanted to do nothing but move out there.

I came back to New York, but I didn't dare tell anyone how I felt. So I decided I'd force them to ask me to leave by being morose and dragging things down. For about two weeks I sat around with this ball of yarn and I'd roll it up into a ball and then I'd unwind it again and wrap it around a pipe. I didn't say anything. Tried to be morose. But nobody paid any attention to what I did.

One day I mentioned to Andre that I'd really like to go out to Mexico. He picked up on it right away and said, "No matter where you go I'll come after you and drag you back. You can't escape." Finally the feeling went away.

Gerry: We all had an incredible desire to make the project work. Stronger than a desire really. A need. And it saved us. Kept us together. Andre had been through the alternatives. Larry had been to regional theaters and didn't want to go back. I needed it because I'm a fanatic. Everyone must have felt it in some very deep way, or we would never have survived. We all knew that once we walked out it would be like committing ourselves to limbo forever.

THE MOUSE'S STORY

"Fury said to a mouse that he met in the house, 'Let us both go to law: I will prosecute you . . .''

Gerry: The Caucus Race was the most complex scene we worked on. We just couldn't find out what it meant to go through a Pool of Tears and then run a frantic race, whether that was metaphorical or realistic or what. Andre was sure that once we figured out that scene it would help us find what the rest was all about.

Andre: From the very beginning one of the reasons I'd been so excited about the idea of doing *Alice in Wonderland* was that I knew it would involve the animal work. The Caucus Race chapter was full of animals. I think there may have been as many as eighteen in all. A lot more than we could possibly handle. Each actor chose the animal he wanted to play.

Gerry: We began working on it during the summer, the same period we were working on all the family improvisations. For a while we kept going back and forth between the Liddells and this bunch of animals on a damp desert island.

Angela: In the beginning of the Caucus Race chapter it says that Alice felt she recognized the animals. That they were familiar to her in some way. To me the scene seemed like the first level of sleep. She is dreaming about people she knows—her family and friends—but they appear in disguises. I always felt a very strong connection between the family improvisations and the Caucus Race.

Tommy: I had decided early on that since I was Lewis Carroll in the first scene, I'd be Lewis Carroll all the way through the play. So in rehearsals the idea of a through-line was very important to me. I had failed in the first scene—failed to get Alice to play it my way. So in the Caucus Race I come back as this dumb Dodo, punishing myself for having been so stupid. That's where the Dodo's stutter came from. My head was filled with Lewis Carrollisms which kept popping out in different places.

Andre: I think that Tommy's choosing to be the Dodo had a lot to do with his reluctance to get involved in the physical aspect of the work. The Dodo strikes me as an animal that lives almost entirely in its head. It seems in constant fear of displeasing anyone and moves only with great hesitation. In the family improvisations Tommy was always trying to smooth things over and keep everybody happy.

Tommy: The Dodo is really kind and gentle. He loves Alice.

Angela: He's always coming over to me in the scene. Leaning on me, huddling up against me.

Andre: The animal work we did really took two forms. One was from the inside out. Trying to find the animal in oneself, the physical and emotional center of its life. The thing was to avoid the clichés, to remember that there are ferocious mice and cowardly lions.

Saskia: I think what we kept trying to do was to surprise each other. And ourselves. To think only of what you want and try in any way you can to get it. Stand on your head. Shit. Recite Shakespeare. Anything. Just to get what you want.

Andre: The other thing we did was to go from the outside in: visit a zoo or a pet shop and watch the animal; study its physical nature. And then, by making an extreme commitment to those physical details with our own bodies, discover the associations that come out of it.

Saskia: I had seen a parrot in the window of a jewelry shop. The owner was a seaman. I asked him if I could come and watch his parrot because I was playing a parrot. I would sit there for hours watching that bird. I had always imagined parrots as very asexual, but I could see that whenever the man would scratch the parrot at the edge of its wing, the wing would open up and his head would move around on his neck, it seemed like a hundred and eighty degrees. I was so intrigued by the beak. And that hard little tongue he had. When he would eat he'd put the food in his beak and then crush it with that hard tongue. He looked very much in control, very superior, as long as he was sitting on the bar. But if you put him on the floor, everything changed. He wobbled around looking dumb and silly. He entirely lost his status as soon as he was on the floor. And I think he knew it. He kept trying to get back on the bar.

The thing I found out was when I tried to be that bird, the joints in my knees went in the opposite way the parrot's joints do. I couldn't bend my legs the way I wanted. I got so angry that I couldn't become that parrot. All I could do was what struck me about him. I think it's a condescending bird. Snobbish. Wants to have everything under control. Doesn't like to mingle with other animals. In the first improvisations I was always standing on a chair, trying to get everybody's attention so they would come over to me.

Angela: I have the advantage over Saskia in the Caucus Race. As Alice I'm new to this group of animals, and their attention is on me the whole time. The Lory and I are both vying for the attention of the men.

Saskia: It's true. In this scene Alice does get everybody's attention, and the Lory doesn't. So there was some kind of jealousy there.

Angela: It was a period in which I felt very competitive with Saskia. We were the only two women in the company, and she was still new to the group, while I had been there since the beginning. There was also a time when she really wasn't working at all, and I had been working constantly. Even when Andre wasn't actually dealing with me as an actress, I had to be there as the cheese so other people could do their scenes.

Andre: In addition to being a new member of the group, Saskia wasn't American. I think she felt that very deeply. It was both a problem for her and a point of pride. On top of that she had been playing Alice's sister in the family improvisations, which meant that people were often ignoring her and she had to make a lot of noise in order to get anybody's attention. I think she actually felt a little bit like a noisy, critical bird.

Angela: There's a constant kind of sibling rivalry between the Lory and Alice in the scene.

Andre: Larry had decided to be the Duck. I think his original reason was his Texas Baptist background. According to the *Annotated Alice*, the Duck represents a minister who had been very close to the Liddell family. So it all seemed very logical. The trouble was, Larry found it absolutely impossible to believe in the character of a preacher. And I don't think anyone can play a character he doesn't believe in. But by that time we'd done a lot of work on the scene, and Larry was really stuck with the Duck. It became a question of his finding some other way to do it. What he eventually discovered came out of something physical. He was a duck, so he was squatting most of the time and making these quacking noises which really sounded pretty vulgar. It began to suggest a kind of dirty burlesque comic. He began going after Alice in the scene and making semisuggestive remarks to her. "Hey, baby, why don't you take off your clothes." He must have known it annoyed her. But like all the other animals, the Duck is wet and uncomfortable. And of course one way to try to alleviate one's own discomfort is to annoy someone else. For me the scene had a lot to do with the ways in which one tries to distract oneself from pain.

Gerry: We did a lot of improvisations under an umbrella. What happens to six people—or six animals— stuck on an island with only one umbrella, when the weather is so unfriendly that you can't go out in it.

Andre: It had to do with exploring the past life of the animals, their relationships, the discomfort and isolation of the island. It started out as a kind of game. I said, "You have one umbrella among you. You can't get out from under it because it's raining and your clothes will get wet and you only have one set of clothes, so you've got to stay under there until it stops raining." Then I kept it raining for four hours. Finally people were fainting, dropping, struggling to get other people out of there. Much later, that improvisation led to Jabberwocky.

Larry: I hate the Jabberwock. It is my most unfavorite thing in the play. I had an idea. It was my idea to get under the umbrella and do the poem. I wanted to create the monster, the Jabberwocky monster. I wanted to create a far-out monster with people doing really crazy things. But nobody would do it. Nobody else had my vision. So finally Andre told us each to take a verse. It got to the point where the only thing we could do with it was to try and outscream the other person until we all broke apart.

Angela: It's a wonderful way to begin the performance. We're back behind the paper curtain, all huddled together under the umbrella. And we start preparing back there. For me it's a very secure feeling being together with the group and coming out on stage hidden. It's a wonderful entrance for me. I'm shielded. I'm protected. I'm with my friends.

Larry: I think Jabberwocky is the most like us, the way we are with each other. We just can't come together on it; we always have a hard time agreeing on what's good.

Andre: This bunch of actors can have a terrible time working together in a group scene.

Gerry: The Caucus Race took longer to finish than any scene we worked on except maybe Alice and Lewis. But with the Caucus Race, what kept happening was we'd reach a point where we felt we were off on the wrong track. The only thing to do then was to leave it, and go back to it in a month or so.

Andre: The central idea of the scene was so bleak that the actors hated doing it. Our approach was very realistic. The actors re-created personally uncomfortable environments and experiences. We also used an exercise learned from Grotowski called the Kissing Exercise, which was very similar to the sensory work I had done with Strasberg. You conjure up a very specific sensation on one part of your body, a kiss on your neck, sunlight on your waist, ice on the ball of your foot, and leave yourself open to the responses. Often we combined that with vocal work, so that the actor, concentrating entirely on an imaginary sensation, would suddenly begin to sing. Because he had forgotten about his voice he often discovered an entirely new one. Many of the animal sounds came out of that.

Gerry: It's a process of finding out what you can easily give. At first everyone does what comes easily. Then you start pushing farther and you get to the point where you start doing things that are more difficult, more dangerous, that involve greater risks. It's not finding what your limits are. I defy anybody to do that. It's merely a matter of continually edging out into the unknown. Anybody can do it. Any artist has to. But most actors aren't given the chance.

Andre: When everybody first chose parts for the Caucus Race, Gerry was going to play the young Crab. There are two crabs in the scene. A grandfather Crab, who was Jerry Mayer, and the grandson.

Gerry: I had a famous line. "You're enough to try the patience of an oyster."

Andre: But that left us with no Mouse. And we really needed a Mouse. So Gerry said he would do it.

Angela: He's so fair. He never lets his personal emotions wreck what's best for the group.

Andre: There's something very strange about the Mouse in the Caucus Race. I've always thought of a mouse as a sexually ambivalent creature. A rat was definitely male, but I felt you could never be sure about a mouse. During all the family improvisations in which Gerry was playing the father, there'd been no mother. And in the Caucus Race it's as though he becomes both. One moment he seems like a very weak, frightened father, and the next he is almost like a classic Jewish mother, bemoaning her lot.

Angela: For me it's perfect having Gerry as the dogmatic Mouse. There is that side of him. When Andre is late to a rehearsal and we're all sitting around drinking coffee, Gerry will be up there doing the Plastiques and working out. He's our artistic conscience. He really works. Sticks by all the rules. There are times I think he'd make an ideal Alice.

Andre: The Crab was the most natural choice for Jerry Mayer. Not just because he was a grandfather again. But it seemed natural to his sense of isolation that he chose to play a creature literally imprisoned in its own shell. What happens to him physically in the role, the way his arms are wrapped around his body, it's like someone in a strait jacket. That all came from him.

Jerry: I never felt that Andre put any directorial restraint on me. Everything that happens has a reason behind it. For instance, I discovered in one of the improvisations that, as soon as the Dodo opens his mouth, I've got to find out what's going on over there. The movement I make to get to him I think pleases Andre no end. Not because there's anything special in it, but because I do what he wants. I get over to the other side of the stage. But Andre never told me to go there.

Andre: I hardly ever tell an actor to do anything. I never impose my own ideas. I don't really have any until after I've seen something. Then I know. Somehow I find a way to bring out what's in me through them.

Gerry: Andre always lets you discover things yourself and, from that, finds what he can take that's good and has you expand on it. He almost never says, "No, that's bad." What he likes might be the tiniest, most insignificant thing, but it's something to build on.

Angela: All of a sudden you're not a puppet any more. You don't have to worry about trying to fit yourself into some crazy concept in a director's mind. You have to use yourself, your own responses, things that are true to your nature.

Andre: I like to think I'm being so democratic in allowing the actor to do whatever he wants, only very delicately and politely suggesting that this might be better than that. Refining things. But it may be the most egotistical way to be a director. I mean, everyone knows that directors like to play god. Well, there are small gods and big gods. The small gods have to show their power so they move people around a lot and lay down the rules. But what could be more egotistical and closer to the image of god than to be completely absent? That to me is the cruelest and most interesting god of all.

Jerry: All the moves people make in that scene really please Andre. But I don't recall his ever saying, "I want you to go from here over to there." After we found it he would often say, "Remember that, let's keep it." Like at the end of the race where I say, "Who won, who who who," skittering across the stage, I discovered that one day in the improvisations, and then, months later, the movement I made started to change and Andre told me to go back to it. And toward the end he tightened things up a bit. When we were in a clump he'd ask us to be a little closer together. But it sure never felt like direction to me.

Andre: What finally happened in this scene was that we were able to get the animals, we were able to get the pain, the isolation, the games, and the frenzied race. But we couldn't get any order. In the end I had to block it. But that blocking never could have had any logic if the actors hadn't first stumbled through it.

What amazes me — and it's true of all my productions — is the sense of movement. I feel I couldn't stage my way out of a paper bag. But every one of my productions has been extremely physical, even in as contained a world as *Endgame:* it was as physical as you could possibly be, paralyzed in a trashcan.

When a production is finished and I look at it, it always makes me wonder. It seems so staged, so choreographed. And it's particularly weird in *Alice.* The sense of movement and fluid pictures. Because it's the most staged of anything I've ever done, and yet in a funny way it's the one I'm the most absent from. That's a real mystery to me. Because I know the actors can't have done it themselves. At least I think not. But I'm sure I didn't do it.

Larry: Those were two hard years. NYU had given us a room which was called 3-D—third dimension. And there we were. In the same building where we'd all gone to school. The six of us. We'd been the first students when the NYU School of the Arts was formed, and had supposedly been the best class, and there we were like ghosts haunting the building. Not in school, but in a way not out of it, either.

Jerry: In the beginning, when we all decided to stay together, I thought we'd take a few months to put a show together, open it, and see what happened. I couldn't conceive of it taking any longer. From the beginning we paid lip service to the idea of creating a company. But I don't think you can really look on it in those terms while you're working. You think, Tomorrow I have to be there at nine-thirty and we're going to be doing those damned exercises again. Then you go home at night and have your fantasies about the results.

Andre: I sometimes think they had the feeling that there wasn't any director, that there was simply some kind of maniac who kept showing up. But I insisted that we work as a group. That's very rare and it puts enormous burdens on everyone.

Gerry: A lot of what we did was completely thrown out—chapters like Tweedledum and Tweedledee, and Wool and Water. We spent about two months on each of them, then decided they wouldn't work and dropped them. I think we did almost as much work on The Rabbit Sends a Little Bill as we did on the Mad Tea Party, but the scene is now only about a minute long.

Larry: The Rabbit Sends a Little Bill is the chapter where the White Rabbit mistakes Alice for his maid and sends her to fetch his gloves, and she goes in the house and eats cookies and gets big and then they burn the house down.

Andre: I loved it because it seemed really terrifying, and involved Alice's getting big again.

Larry: We'd been trying to do it as a radio show, with the five of us sitting around a table. I was the announcer, and Alice was out in the middle as if she were listening to a radio program. The idea was that the person listening would experience all the things that were coming over the radio, but there would be no human contact. The rule was that we couldn't go forward in the program until all five of us behind the table were convinced that the person listening had really gone through the whole experience we were laying out.

Andre: The people behind the table were like grand inquisitors. Their objective was to make Alice shrink emotionally. They used the lines from the texts, but underneath the words there was always some secret accusation. During these improvisations different people became Alice.

Larry: I remember one time Saskia was Alice. She was out there listening. We kept trying to get through to her, but she was just sitting there making her disgusting noises. Nothing was happening, so we were stuck. Finally, after about three hours of this, Tom couldn't stand it any more. He gritted his teeth and said, "They threw rocks at her and she stuck them up her ass and they came out in little cakes." We all looked at one another and burst out laughing. It wasn't really all that funny, but we were so mad at Saskia it seemed hilarious. We must have laughed for an hour and a half. Poor Saskia never understood what it was all about. Her feelings were hurt.

Andre: In the end we chose only what seemed to us the most terrifying lines in the chapter and condensed the scene to less than a minute. We had a private logic for ourselves connecting the scenes. In Little Bill it came out of the fact that Alice had just frightened the animals at the end of the Caucus Race by talking about her cat. So, as a kind of revenge, they came back as nightmare figures and put her through an awful experience, trapping her in a house and burning it down around her.

Saskia: The worst part for me came in September when Andre started to work on the Mad Tea Party. I had nothing to do. Nothing except the Lory. I would sit in my room for days. I didn't know where to start with the Lory, and I couldn't work with Andre. Then we would read in the paper that he was going to direct at Lincoln Center or at Yale and we never heard from him. So I was really very suspicious of him. I kept wondering, "Who is this man? Is he a big fake?"

Gerry: Jerry Mayer and Saskia were both getting increasingly difficult to work with—which doubtless had a lot to do with the fact that it was Andre's worst period, too. Saskia was coming in late. She was still having a lot of trouble feeling part of the group. She was very defensive, and didn't trust Andre at all.

Angela: Andre used to call me up and we'd go for coffee. He was very upset about the whole thing. Jerry was constantly bucking him. He'd say things like, "Just give me my blocking." That kind of actor. Not believing in this method. With Saskia it was the opposite. She could improvise constantly, but if she found something good, she could never hold onto it.

Gerry: Andre finally threw up his hands in despair. He didn't know how to deal with Jerry and Saskia. He came to me, and the two of us had a long talk about it. He kept saying, "What am I going to do? I don't feel we can get anywhere. Do I ask them to quit? What can I do?" I didn't know the answer.

Larry: For months Saskia had been going along in her way, making her noises and doing all this off-the-wall shit. Andre finally came to feel it was off the wall, too. Things got to the point that Saskia wasn't doing her work. And Andre wasn't working with her. He simply ignored her.

Saskia: Maybe it was because he felt I was too dependent on him. I had nothing except that group, and I couldn't work. So I leaned on him. I couldn't get myself to feel that I was an actress. I told myself that, no matter what happened. I would keep on working, even if I have to do it all by myself. I'd do a monologue. Anything. But I couldn't. I did nothing instead.

Larry: You have to be alive for Andre. You have to be constantly giving him something to pick and choose from. When you don't he gets uptight.

Andre: Saskia came into the group with a great knowledge of Grotowski's work, and Peter Brooks'; she talked about how she dreamed of a totally independent actor, one who created for himself, with the director as a kind of guide but with the actor really on his own. That puts a huge burden of responsibility on each person's shoulders. I think that when I created that situation for Saskia, she nearly went mad.

Larry: Andre is never one to ask someone to leave; he's one to just make things happen. But Saskia's so hard-headed and single-minded, she hung in there. Stayed through it. But she had a hard time for a while, going through all kinds of paranoia, thinking people in the company didn't like her because she wasn't an American. Crazy things like that.

Saskia: Like everybody else, I thought of leaving. But I have this Calvinistic attitude; I have to finish what I start.

Larry: It's hard to make Andre mad, but when it happens it's very unpleasant. He doesn't yell. He's very quiet. But he calls you a 42nd Street pimp. Fishwife. Things like that. You hate to see him mad. It's very upsetting. Very upsetting.

Gerry: One day he came in and blew his cool. Really harangued us. It was like he'd been storing it up for months and it had all become exaggerated and he just let it all out.

Saskia: When Andre does get mad he's a real tongue-lasher. He doesn't cry or yell or throw things. He just sits there and goes bat-bat-bat with words. He did that at me one day. He was irrational. He said I was lazy. Called me perverted. An ugly fishwife. Terrible things.

Gerry: He said Saskia was just being original for the sake of being original. That Jerry Mayer was impossible to work with. That none of us cared about the theater because we never read anything. Never went to see anything.

Saskia: I felt so defenseless. I didn't know how to answer him. All I said was, "I don't think you should talk like that to me, because you make it immediately into a director-actress relationship. You're setting up an inferiority and superiority thing with me." And Gerry Bamman told him he was talking bullshit.

Gerry: We answered back. I was so pissed-off at his saying none of us went to the theater that I could hardly see straight. At the time we were averaging twenty-five dollars a week, and I was driving a cab four nights a week just to live. So I had hardly any time, let alone the money, to go to the theater. The point was, you answered back. You didn't give in.

Larry: The fights you usually have in the theater last a split-second. You scream and yell at each other, go off and pout a while, come back, and it's, "Oh darling, it's all better. I'm sorry." But inside you're still pissed-off. With us that's not allowed to ferment. The work forces it to come out, and when it does, something gets done to allay those hang-ups so we can get on with the work. Because that was always everyone's main concern. The work itself.

Gerry: That was the only time in the entire two years that Andre blew up like that. And when it was over, it was really over. I consider that a pretty good track record. What was on everybody's mind was that if it was going to work none of us could be the one to give in. I think the only way any of the six of us would leave is if we ran out the door screaming, right into a strait jacket.

Larry: Andre had promised us that we would put the show on in March, and we all felt we had to stick it out till then. As it happened, we didn't open in March, but by that time we had figured out some other reason to stay together.

THE CATERPILLAR

"You just wait . . . you're going to have to change into a chrysalis . . . and after that into a butterfly. You'll find that a little queer . . . . won't you?"

Larry: Tom Costello had been working on the Caterpillar for a long time. I started watching it in rehearsals. I didn't like the way he was doing it. He was doing it as this Maharishi-type person. Talked like the Maharishi. Sat there with his eyes wide open. And the thing was, he didn't let anything really affect him. It was as though he had some sort of super-knowledge, and from his lofty position he kept telling Alice all sorts of things. I kept thinking, "Now if this guy has been sitting around smoking all this time, he must be stoned out of his gourd." I guess that's why I had a thing for doing the Caterpillar. I kept seeing him as this guy who was so stoned he couldn't see straight. So I started saying to Andre, "Hmm, the Caterpillar. I'd like to do the Caterpillar." One day Andre said, "Why don't you do it." So I did.

Andre: We began with a three-part Caterpillar made of Larry, Tommy, and Jerry Mayer. They sat on stools, one behind the other, with Larry in front.

Larry: I was the intellect. Tom was the emotional. Jerry was the sexual.

Andre: This Caterpillar was at war with itself. It had six arms, and it was constantly tearing itself apart.

Larry: I would say things and then Tommy or Jerry would echo what I said.

Andre: There were three different voices: Larry's natural voice, Tommy's Indian voice, and Jerry Mayer's low sexual groan. So it was very musical. We did it like that for about four months and it was a beautiful piece of work. But I guess Larry never liked it.

Larry: It had some pretty good things in it, but I was always unhappy with it. Every time I would get something going, they would fuck it up. I'd be working on something and a hand would come around and start grabbing at me and I could never get anywhere. I nearly got ulcers over it.

THE MUSHROOM

"One side makes
you grow taller and the
other side makes you grow smaller.
The Mushroom!"

Andre: Larry kept mentioning the idea of making the Mushroom out of the other actors. For a long time I wouldn't listen. I really never let him finish. I don't know why I was so against it. I think it reminded me of an African throne made of human bodies I'd once done in another production.

Larry: One day, to get over my ulcers I guess, I just did it. I made the Mushroom, got on top of it. "How do you like this, Andre?" He said, "Okay."

Andre: Larry had to fight to get us to accept his idea of the Mushroom. He really prefers to pretend he's not very intelligent or articulate, but he was forced to use that part of himself. He had to defend what was basically a directorial idea.

Angela: Larry likes to masquerade as a dumb country boy from Texas who doesn't know anything.

Andre: He was absolutely right about the Mushroom. It was sheer genius. The whole thing with the stools, even though it had nice moments, would have been clumsy and conventional.

Larry: Andre says that one of the nice things about the group now is that all the actors are in a way directors, too. In *Alice,* each of us contributed different parts, scenic things. Andre would only choose.

Andre: I needed actors who could think as well as feel.

Larry: You do a scene for another director and he says, "Okay, where were you coming from? Where are you going? What do you want?" When you work with Andre you don't really have to be coming from anywhere. You can find out in the work where you came from.

Andre: So what am I there? I'm like an eye, some kind of eye that knows what it wants only when that becomes visible.

Angela: Larry is always saying to Andre, "I don't know what I do or how I do it. I don't know anything. I have no technique." But when you watch him work, you can see that's not true. He knows damn well what he's doing.

Larry: In the beginning my objective, my super-objective through the whole play, was to change Angela Pietropinto and turn her on a little bit. Get her to stop clutching at all her tiny little things. Get her to stop bullshitting in the bourgeois way she has. It sounds stupid, I know, but that's what I was doing. But I found out it was impossible, and it's hard to work on something you know is impossible. So I had to find something else. Now what I want to do is just give her a hard time. Every time she thinks she's got hold of something logical and I have a chance to fuck that logic up, I'll zoom in and try to twist it around for her. And it's me doing all these things in the guise of being this stoned Caterpillar or being the Dormouse. Just to put her on this trip.

Jerry: Larry Pine is the most perfectly intuitive actor I have ever seen.

Tommy: I love Larry. I've never loved anybody like I love Larry. I remember long before we ever got into this company I saw him rehearsing a scene one day. It was a scene from Shaw. The fantastic thing was that he was doing it as himself, this Texas kid, not hiding behind anything. He made no attempt to characterize the part. I was really impressed.

Angela: With Larry I'm always surprised. I don't really know him. He doesn't let you really into him. I think I understand the others fairly well, but Larry always surprises me. And I feel that the Caterpillar is the first weird, fantastical encounter for Alice.

Larry: When Alice comes on, my job is to fuck her head up. Every time she thinks she's doing something right I've got to say, No, that's all wrong. I start out trying to make her believe in me. Asking her who she is, that sort of thing. And when she's feeling a little sure of herself, I fuck her up.

Angela: I have to try to leave myself open. I've got to trust him. I've got to find some way to make myself believe each time that tonight it will be different.

Larry: Working on a new thing, rehearsing something new, is very important to keeping the performances of *Alice* alive. If we stop working together we begin losing interest in each other. That's the whole secret of this play. It's an event. There's a whole life created out there and it comes out of doing things with each other. You can't fake that.

Angela: I never thought of Larry as being especially attractive when I first met him. I'm the kind of woman who doesn't care what a man looks like; it's what he's done, what his ideals are, his views. Then I get turned on. It took me a while to see through Larry's dumb-country-boy thing. When I did, I began to find him more attractive, and that affects what happens between us in the scene.

Larry: I can't ever remember using a relationship I had with anyone in the group. They change all the time. I work on relationships I've had with other people. I can't count on a feeling I might have about someone in the group to work all the time. With Angela, that time when I was happy she was leaving; that wouldn't work now. Because now I wouldn't be happy to see her leave.

Angela: Larry's trying to get something out of me when he's the Caterpillar. I'm not sure really what it is. We don't tell each other these things. But I think I thwart him.

Larry: This is the only play I've ever been in where I'm nervous every night because I'm not sure. I'm not sure I know what I'm doing. In any straight play you finally get to the point where you can do it with your eyes closed. But in this one you can't. It's so tenuous. And sometimes what it hangs on just disappears.

————————

Andre: I suppose everyone has certain obsessions about his childhood. I had a very strong picture of myself as an unwanted child, knocked about a lot by the adults around me. Pig and Pepper instantly struck me as very personal. It seemed like a great scene for me to express some of the feelings I had about that kind of household and that kind of childhood.

Saskia: I worked on the Duchess in Pig and Pepper for a long time from a psychological point of view and got absolutely nowhere. I was thinking about it conventionally, about a mother with a baby. But of course we weren't using a real baby in the scene. It was just a doll. And I don't know what it is to have a baby. I am not a mother. Why should I pretend to be one? So for a long time I was very lost with that scene.

Andre: In the beginning we worked on the scene in a conventional, realistic way. Everybody in the house had a specific objective. The Duchess wanted to get rid of the baby so she could get out into the social world. The Cat was starved for affection and wanted to kill the baby because he saw the baby as his rival. The Cook wanted to kill the baby and cook it, I can't remember why.

Tommy: We did so many improvisations for that scene. At one point I think I was a cat who was a prisoner and would be punished if he ceased to smile. Then I was a cat who kept licking himself because he loved himself so much. Then I was really the Duchess' husband, reduced to the status of a pet because he was impotent.

Andre: We kept making certain assumptions to explain the fact that there was no father in the house. For a while we thought maybe the Frog Footman was the father who had been kicked out of the house and turned into a servant by the Duchess. We explored the possibility that the Cook was the Duchess' rejected lover. None of these assumptions got us very far.

Saskia: They were very cruel improvisations. Larry was playing the Cook and he was always throwing things at the rest of us. I think for a while we were even using a real butcher knife.

Andre: I think it's natural to the acting process to begin with excesses. Violence. Sexuality. Somehow those are always the first things you go to.

Larry: We threw out more shit. I mean Andre can sit and watch anything. Anything. For hours and hours.

Jerry: And really watch it. If it was funny he'd be rolling in the aisles. If it was sad he'd be crying. That's really hard. I couldn't do it.

Andre: It was as if the actors were constantly trying it out in front of an audience. An audience of one. And when they got a response, they knew they had something.

Larry: But there were times when we'd spend four and five hours on an improvisation and it would lead, as far as I was concerned, absolutely nowhere.

Tommy: It can be maddening. I mean, I always used to feature myself as the dramaturge. I was very intellectual about the whole thing. Always picking up these little character facets. In the book the Cat keeps disappearing, so one day I decided that nobody pays any attention to you as an actor if there's no thought in your head. I figured out that the Cat's disappearance would merely be a relaxation starting from the forehead and going down until the smile relaxes and he's totally relaxed in the middle of the stage. I kept getting little ideas like that, and I'd talk to Andre about them, and he'd say, "Great. Beautiful. Do it." And long beyond my interest in it, he'd keep me doing it until it would become a kind of trap and I'd say, "Hey, that was a stupid idea!" And maybe out of all of it would come one tiny gesture you'd keep.

Larry: Even if nothing very dramatic happens, you start to build up a lot of feelings about being together in that situation.

Saskia: What I hate about the conventional theater is that you feel, watching the actors, that they are pretending. It's like the *Reader's Digest* coming to life. It's silly psychology. And therefore it's dull. Because it's glutted with generalities.

Larry: I suspect that if Andre wasn't there we would all fall into the trap of staying inside ourselves. In a lot of theater today, the actors are only talking to themselves, and therefore they bore the hell out of everybody else. They probably have a lot of juices going inside their own bodies, but they don't come out and affect anybody else. That's one thing Andre's always understood: that energy isn't any good unless it's flowing out toward other things.

Andre: Acting is action. Wanting something and reaching out for it. If in reaching out you get what you want or fail to get what you want, that experience may produce an emotion. But to search for the emotion is working ass-backwards. You can't assume an emotion or invent one. All you can do is be open to it when it comes to you.

Tommy: I'm always looking for the key. I remember once as a kid I was playing around with theater in high school, and one time I did a role and everything worked right. About halfway through the performance I realized that these people were paying attention to me in such a way that if I smiled, they would smile. Man, what a feeling. And ever since then I've been trying to figure out how that happened. Trying to put a method on it. I suppose the only method is to forget it and just be there, really be there every minute. But that's harder, that's much harder.

Gerry: You can never know in advance the right way to work. It doesn't matter so much what you do. The important thing is to do something. It's like the Cheshire Cat saying to Alice, "If you walk far enough, you're bound to get somewhere." But no one can tell you in what direction to walk.

Saskia: Doing Pig and Pepper in a psychological way made it clear we could only go so far. But we felt the scene was deeper than that. It was not only a scene about a repressed household.

Andre: We had started working on the Mad Tea Party and we had been using the table in that part. Somebody came up with the idea of cramming the whole Pig and Pepper household under the table. That helped a lot, because it made the scene truly claustrophobic. But it still felt incomplete.

Shortly before we were supposed to open at the Loft in New Jersey in April 1970, I came up with the idea that the people under the table could be figments of Alice's speed hallucinations. She had just eaten the Mushroom, so she must be on a trip and she sees all these people as mechanical toys in which the machinery had gone wild.

Tommy: The mechanical cat was really an inspiration. We'd worked on the scene so long, I just went crazy one day and turned into this mechanical cat. I find mechanical contrivances awfully frightening. The mechanical cat is one of my favorite things in the play, except for the fact that it's never really worked right since that first day. I think I must be self-conscious about it.

Andre: The idea of the mechanical toys had an immediate effect on everyone's speech. They started talking about three times faster than normal. And it changed the nature of the gestures, like Larry's cooking and Saskia's rocking the baby.

Saskia: As soon as the others, the Cook and the Cat and the Frog Footman, became mechanical toys, it helped a lot. And of course we had already done all that psychological work, so the mechanical thing was not just superficial.

Tommy: For me it's not that I'm playing at being a mechanical cat. It's what happens to me when I'm confronted with the limitations of a mechanical cat. It's hard to explain. It's myself, always myself, but hiding behind a mechanical cat.

Angela: Pig and Pepper really took me a long time. I felt completely out of that one. Even after we'd performed it for a while I still couldn't make any sense out of it. Then I discovered something out of working with Saskia in the scene.

Saskia: I think that the Duchess is simply very dumb. Her rhythm is slow, and she doesn't understand the things Alice says to her.

Angela: Alice is impressed by the fact that this woman is a Duchess. She's a freaky Duchess all right, but she's still a Duchess. So Alice starts to trot out all her knowledge, intellectual bullshit really, to show off for this woman.

  You see, sometimes I feel I have to prove to Saskia that I have a brain. That I'm not just this little thing depending on the big strong man she married, or on Andre Gregory who, in a way, she also married. When I began using that aspect of my relationship with Saskia in the scene, it worked for me.

Andre: I think it was when we were playing in Cambridge in June that we discovered the game of Hot Potato, in which nobody wants the baby and it is constantly flung from one person to the other.

Tommy: I felt all along that Andre knew exactly what he wanted. And that he was just waiting for us to come up with it ourselves. I used to say that I liked directors who could trick you into it. Andre doesn't trick you into it; he lets your own boredom drive you into it.

Andre: Some people in the company believe that the whole production was in my mind from the very beginning. I have no idea, I really don't, whether that's true or not. I like to think it was. And it's hard for me to understand how the production could be as unified as it is without there having been something in my head to start with. But it's all so mysterious. Because I know many of the things they brought to Alice were things I had never imagined and probably never would have. I just recognized them when I saw them.

Jerry: I haven't the faintest idea how much Andre knew about what the results would be ahead of time. If I were to discover that he didn't have a clue about what it was going to be until we put it together to play in New Jersey, that wouldn't surprise me a bit. On the other hand, if I were to learn that the entire thing was in his head from the moment Angela came up with the idea of *Alice,* I'd believe that, too.

PIG AND PEPPER

''I speak severely to my boy and beat him when he sneezes, for he can thoroughly enjoy the pepper when he pleases.''

THE MAD TEA PARTY

''We quarrelled Time and I some time ago . . . just last March it was . . . just before HE went mad.''

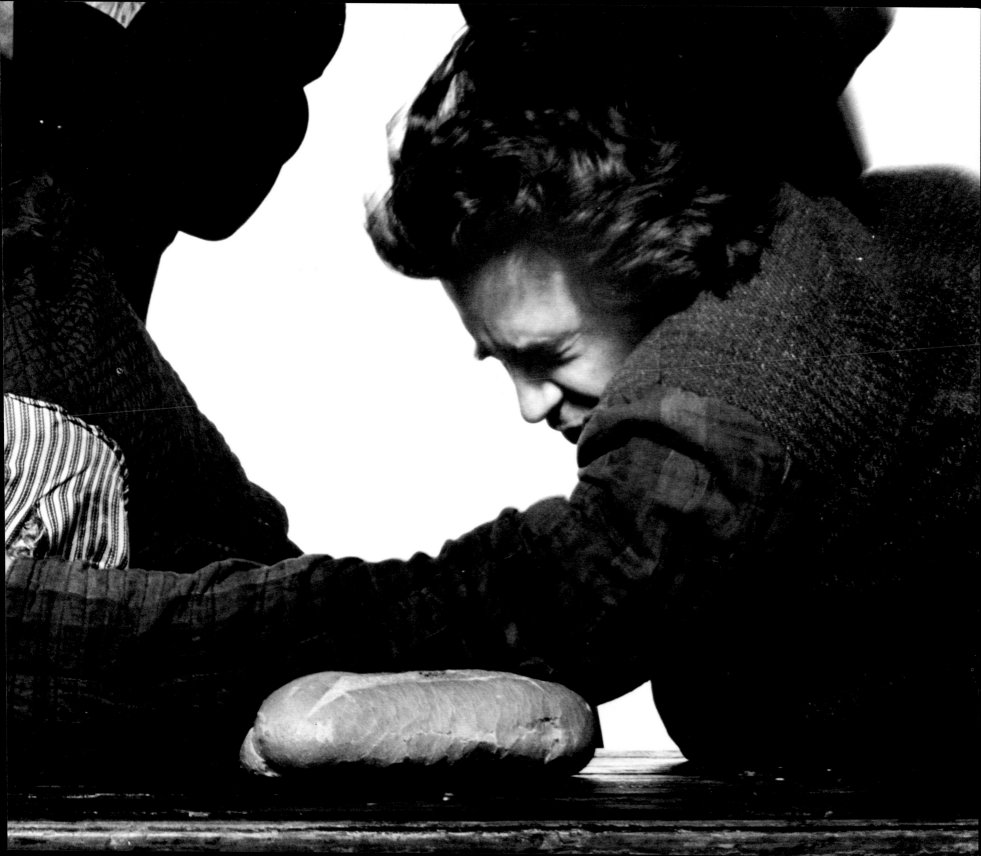

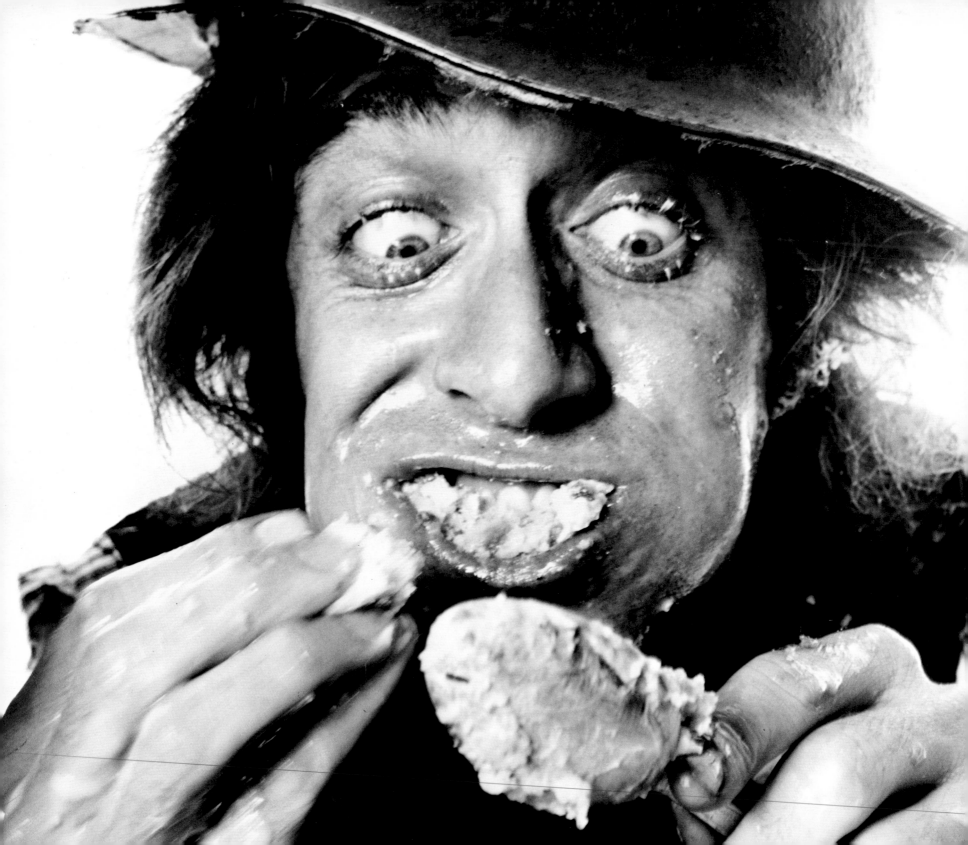

Gerry: I think Jerry Mayer·is probably the most striking
example of Andre's patience. I've seen acting
teachers break their backs over Jerry Mayer and
get nowhere. He has a well-thought-out philosophy
of acting, although he could probably never
articulate it. He has very clear opinions about
what he wants to do. He's very stubborn and relies
only on himself—all of which can be good.
But it can also set up an impenetrable wall
between him and a director.

Andre: Jerry Mayer likes to think of himself as the most
conservative member of the group—politically,
socially, artistically. He just wanted to be told
where to go and what to do. And I absolutely
refused to give that to him. It isn't my way of
working. And so for a year, if that's possible, I
allowed him literally to do nothing and watch
everybody else doing things. Finally he exploded.

Jerry: We were rehearsing the Mad Tea Party and did
a lot of improvisations with the Mad Hatter, the
Dormouse, and the March Hare before Alice ever
shows up. The improvisations lasted a long time,
four and five hours each day. And they were
insane. Really wild.

Gerry: Andre is very cunning. He's so aware of all the
complexities of a situation that he refuses to
simplify it; he won't commit himself until he has
had a chance to see where it's going. That's the
way he works as a director. That quality makes
him the most fascinating director I've ever known.
And his endurance is phenomenal. He can wait
interminably for you to begin to move and find
your own way.

Andre: For me directing is like fishing. I love to fish.
You're in a quiet place. It's sunset. There are fish
in the water and you throw out the bait and wait.
Wait until you feel something. That's what I do.

**THE
DORMOUSE**

''You might just as well
say that I see what
I eat, is the same thing as
I eat what I see.''

I drop a lure and wait for someone to bite. I just watch. That's why my improvisations sometimes go on for three and four hours. I'm just waiting for someone to bite.

Larry: Anyway, we began the rehearsals for the Tea Party. Jerry Mayer and Gerry Bammam and I used to sit around that table. We started with absolutely nothing. Just a table and three of us sitting around it. Nothing. We didn't even have any words, because Alice wasn't there, so we couldn't use the words in the text. We just sat at that table until the three of us literally went crazy.

Andre: In those rehearsals, Larry and Gerry Bamman tended to go absolutely wild. Larry kept telling stories that were so scatological a marine lieutenant couldn't have done better. And the two of them acted out some incredible fantasies in that room, because there were no women around. It was like a prison.

Gerry: We would work at all hours to see what it was like at night, what it was like early in the morning. They were some of the most obscene, most scurrilous rehearsals we had ever experienced. One day Andre came in with a deck of playing cards from a 42nd Street pornographic book store. Larry got to play with them but Jerry Mayer was never allowed to see them.

Larry: We poured out all kinds of really raunchy filth. At one point I got so sick of being vulgar and filthy that I decided to search for nirvana and wouldn't talk for about a week. I'd just sing the heavenly chord whenever anybody tried to lay anything bad on me.

It got to the point where we didn't even work toward any specific end. We just gathered at that table, and the minute the three of us were there it was like a light bulb going on, you would feel certain pressures and tensions among the three people sitting at the table.

Andre: And through all of it Jerry remained totally apathetic. Finally, one Sunday during a rehearsal, I got desperate and asked him what he felt he needed more than anything from the group. His answer was, "Order." He said he felt that the group had no sense of direction, that it would never get a play finished, that the improvisations went absolutely nowhere, and that everyone was insane except him. So I said, "Okay, your objective at this table is to keep order."

Jerry: I don't think the Mad Hatter's mad. He's upset. But with good reason, from my point of view. You should see some of the things Gerry and Larry were doing in those improvisations. Anyway, we began to discover that the Hatter's main objective in the whole thing was . . . everybody sit down, quiet. We'll drink the tea. Nobody curses. Nobody tells dirty stories. Nobody fights. Just everybody quiet and calm and peaceful. The only problem was that the Dormouse and the Hare had something diametrically opposed in their minds.

Andre: As soon as Jerry tried to keep order he went out of his mind, because it was impossible. Each time the other two would do something wild he would try to calm them down, to keep it orderly and cool and rational.

Jerry: The improvisation had been going on for hours, and I wasn't controlling either Larry or Gerry. I wasn't keeping either one of them decent. I'd been sitting there in my chair, telling them to knock it off, but they weren't listening. They weren't paying any attention to me.

Andre: The more he tried to keep things rational, the more the irrational impulses opened up in him, until finally at one moment he was like a car throbbing violently: his whole body started to hum and throb and shake at the table. And all of a sudden he just lifted the table into the air, this huge table, much heavier than the one we have because it was made of metal, and he hurled it across the room into the wall.

Jerry: I scared the shit out of them. I don't know if I really scared Gerry and Larry, but I scared their characters. I convinced them that if they didn't behave I'd kill them. It wasn't really that I wanted to kill them. My anger wasn't directed toward anyone but myself really. But I sure wanted to destroy the world of that scene. And still do. I mean, there are certain things that Larry did during those rehearsals which, if he ever does them during the show, he's a dead man. That moment in rehearsal of turning over the table, which we kept in the show, was a total release for me. I let everything out. Shocked and amazed my fellow actors. Made Andre very happy.

Andre: I always had the feeling about Jerry Mayer that once when he was young as an actor something happened that made him distrust his behavior. And to protect himself he had taken that behavior and started commenting on it. He developed a form without content. Mannerisms that he put on without going through the process.

Gerry: I think what he does now is incredibly powerful. I don't think he could ever have found those things without Andre. He says so himself. That if he had never met Andre he would have been the kind of actor who relies solely on tricks.

Jerry: I don't know if I can really explain what happened. I just had to control things. And I'm not talking about that scene. Not only as a character, but as an actor. As a human being. I discovered that about myself. I need to control things that I'm involved in. Not necessarily by giving orders. I mean, I decide when I'm in jeopardy.
   So I went mad. And I think Gerry and Larry would agree that there's a very strong possibility I might go berserk as the Hatter. I don't. The things that I do in the play right now are sufficient force to meet the provocation, but if Larry were

to pull his pants down, or if Gerry were to throw Angela down on the table and try to take her pants off and try to screw her, I would go berserk.

Gerry: In what Jerry has found he's able to deal with his own kind of madness. Andre doesn't try to rid Jerry of the things that torment him. He constructs a situation in which Jerry can admit them freely. Revealing your own madness is a very difficult thing for an actor to do. Usually he evades it by pretending to possess someone else's madness, his character's madness.

Andre: The thing about this way of working is that it's potentially very dangerous. The director has to be like a bullfighter. Somewhere he must be able to know when there's a real element of danger. Because sometimes there is. Most often, though, an actor has a wonderful internal mechanism that permits him to go bananas without hurting himself or anyone else. And with Jerry, somehow I knew it was okay.

Jerry: Throwing that table worked. They sat down, by God! They were sitting at that table in no time at all. And now they do what I tell them. I mean they don't really. Getting outside the scene, for a minute, I know they don't. I know that Gerry and Angela are playing footsie under the table, but the Hatter doesn't know it. I know that they are doing things which, if I *allowed* myself to notice them, would upset me. But basically, when I say shut up, they shut up. When I say sit down, they sit down.

And while I'm doing that, the Hare, the son of a bitch, cons me into thinking Alice is going to tell us a story, and it turns out to be Larry, the Dormouse, telling his filthy joke.

We've got a code in that scene. No one could know about it because we developed it in the course of all those improvisations. But the story that Larry tells about Elsie, Lacey, and Tillie is a gross, ugly, vile joke.

Andre: Nobody but those three men and I will ever know the real meaning of Elsie, Lacey, and Tillie.

Jerry: We went through a series of improvisations where he told dirty jokes. And Larry knows some of the ugliest dirty jokes you have ever heard in your life.

Larry: One time Andre went out into the hall while the three of us were sitting at the table, and he brought in some chick from outside. She came in and we just blew her mind. We did her totally. She was in tears by the time we finished. She had to run out. And as she was leaving she turned and said, "This is the most stupid, horrible thing I've ever seen." That's precisely what Alice says when she splits the Tea Party. And I guess Andre felt we were then ready for Alice because shortly after that she came in.

Angela: I was always taught that you have your text and you work on it at home. I can't do this work at home. I work for Andre's eyes. All you can do at home is learn your lines and learn them without thinking. Because if you think about them at home alone you come up with your first answer and it's probably the answer the audience would come up with, too. But if you find something in an improvisation the meaning emerges right out of what you're doing. That's exciting. That's a real discovery.

Andre: I really did something very bizarre with Angela. The logical thing would have been for me to deal with her first. Instead, I didn't deal with her at all. I did everybody else and left Angela alone. It must have been incredibly frustrating for her. All I did was use her for the other people. I'd build the Mad Tea Party, bring her in, and she wouldn't know what she was supposed to do, why she had come there, what she wanted.

Angela: Alice responds to these people, so you have to develop the people first. Andre kept saying, "Leave yourself open." He wanted me to react rather than initiate.

Andre: I can't remember if I did that to her with a purpose or not, but I think it was good for her. It forced her to be truly impulsive. It's a strong quality of hers anyway, one I liked from the beginning, but it became much fuller as a result of my leaving her in the dark. In that way, what Angela went through was very similar to what happened to Alice.

Angela: We would get into the improvisations, and they'd become really wild, like Larry and Gerry would be having a crazy spitting contest, and right in the middle of it Andre would say, "Go to the text." You think to yourself, "He must be crazy." But the minute you do that you begin to discover a whole new logic in what you're saying. Lines which are static when you read the book suddenly begin making sense. They take on a whole new meaning. In the Mad Hatter, for instance, that whole speech about time—"He won't stand beating." He's talking about time. He's also talking about himself. And that's because something was really happening to Jerry when he said those lines.

Andre: We never change the physical details in the play. They are fixed. It was something I think we learned from the Plastique exercises. Since those details and physical actions have come out of deeply personal impulses, they come in some way from a deep part of the actor. If those details remain the same, even though the original impulse may not be there any more, because the actor has changed, the gesture itself is imbued with a personal statement and it can help the actor to give it a new meaning.

Jerry: The audience doesn't affect the Tea Party at all; and I don't think it can. At one point I tried to hold for the audience's laughter, but Andre finally convinced me there was no use in doing that, that there was no need. From the time the butter hits Larry in the mouth the audience is generally noisy, and I keep going no matter what the reaction is.

Andre: Some people get upset because they can't hear everything that's said. But the life of this play is what's important. That's what theater should be. I don't think the theater is literary. It's not verbal. It's something living.

Angela: The Tea Party is great. As a woman in a male world, I love all that attention. The three of them are competing for my attention in such wonderful ways. And I can go anywhere I like. If I'm angry at Gerry Bamman I can give myself to Larry. Or if I'm feeling very motherly toward Jerry Mayer, I can focus on him. And it works. If I give too much attention to Gerry Bamman, Larry gets even crazier. If I lean toward Larry, Gerry Bamman gets more hostile.

And there I don't feel like the cheese. Even though they're the crazy ones, even though they're the ones who are getting the laughs, I'm the one who modulates it.

Andre: I never take notes on Angela's performance any more. My notes are always for the other people. That means her performance has been good. When it isn't, if she's ill and can't surmount it — sometimes she's used being sick to make new discoveries — but if for any reason she isn't able to give herself fully, the entire fabric of the play falls apart. It's only happened a couple of times, but it's devastating. I think it has a lot to do with the fact that her performance is profoundly simple. It keeps it all together.

Angela: I do feel a great responsibility toward the show. Often when the performance is down, it can be traced back to me. Andre has said so. Because, after all, I'm there the whole time. I'm at the center. And if I'm not really responding it can throw everybody off.

Andre: Angela has a terrific coarse American humor throughout the play. It's why some people hate her performance. They find it uncultured. But it's accurate. It's true to the games throughout the play and to the whole quality of the Mad Tea Party.

Angela: It's weird. My New York accent gets very heavy with Alice. Heavier than it is normally. Which comes out of letting down all the barriers. I wasn't aware of it for a long time until reviewers kept pointing it out. When I asked Andre about it, he said, "Oh, it's a brilliant choice!" Well, it wasn't a choice. It just happened.

Andre: I think the Mad Tea Party is the greatest scene we do. It's the purest. The kind of slapstick that pervades that scene is uniquely American. It belongs to borscht belt humor. Other moments in the production are filled with things that can be traced to a European heritage: the physicalization of an imaginary object in making Humpty Dumpty or in forming the Mushroom; or the White Knight scene, which has its roots in the Moscow Art Theater. The building of the Neat Little House can be traced to the work of the Living Theater and further back to the Ballet Béjart. But the comedy in the Tea Party, the extension of anxiety into the crudest form of slapstick theater, is uniquely American.

_____

Larry: After about a year we decided we needed more space so we moved out of 3-D into a loft on Bleeker Street. One day some guy from New Brunswick calls and says, "I hear you people have been doing some fantastic work. Why don't you open it at this theater out here?" You've got to understand, at this point we had no play. We had bits and pieces of things, but we had no play. Not even a beginning. Andre kept saying, "That's okay. We'll think of something." We had a week to think of something.

Gerry: This company is really a result of Andre's personality. We became like a stream flowing in its bed, and if we encountered an obstacle we couldn't surmount, we just went around it.

Andre: There came a point in the work when I felt the room was filled with thousands of sketches, and all we had to do was to find the one we needed. There was a wealth of discarded sketches, and among them an answer to each of our problems.

Larry: So Andre said, "Okay, let's just start the play." We all got up against the wall, and I was sitting there thinking about how to start the play and I started tapping the floor with my foot. Then all of a sudden I started getting a heartbeat out of it. And then I started beating on my chest. Then I got onto my knees and started beating on the floor, Da-*da*, da-*da*, da-*da*. Meanwhile Tom Costello— for some reason his job was to make the Rabbit —grabbed Gerry Bamman and started molding this Rabbit while I was making the heartbeats. We had a Rabbit but nowhere to go. We had to find a hole.

Then I got an idea. We all formed a huddle and became the hole, and Bamman did that fake running and every once in a while the huddle of us would jump so it seemed like he was moving in the hole. Well, that didn't work. After three days looking for a hole and thinking about it I finally said, "Forget it. I'll take it upon myself to make a hole." I had no idea what I was going to do.

I don't know where it came from, but I simply made this hole between my fingers and said, "That's a hole." And then I cracked it open and made this big hole between my legs and bent over and there it was. A hole.

Andre: These actors have been marvelously trained. They work so fast. You can say the tiniest thing to them and they take off.

Larry: We needed a fall. We kept saying, "Okay now, what's a fall?" So we invented a falling exercise called One-Point Balance where you're always only on one point of your body. It could possibly give the illusion you were falling, but it didn't seem quite right.

Andre: It was an exercise Gerry Bamman worked out with the group while I was up at Yale.

Larry: Then we tried having Alice stand in the center, with everybody else at different corners of the room, and we would run toward her and jump over her head, turning somersaults. But Jerry Mayer hurt his back doing that one, which is why he's not in the fall: he was out of commission while we were working on it.

Andre: I'd say, "Well, I don't know. I'd like something a little more mysterious." So then they'd go and do something that was like the prow of a ship. And I'd say, "Well, yeah, a ship's kind of interesting." They know that when I say, "That's kind of interesting," I mean that it's really terrible.

Larry: Somebody came up with the idea of carrying Angela around and sort of dropping and catching her. And we kept saying, "Okay, Angela, shut your eyes and tell us when you feel you're falling so we'll know it's a good thing."

Andre: We were convinced that if only we could make Alice really feel she was falling the audience would believe it, too.

Larry: Finally it evolved into something like a children's game where one person gets tossed around in a circle. Only we took that one person and flung her up in the air, swung her around, let her drop. We had a fall. Whew! We had a fall.

———————

Andre: Then there was the problem of the Croquet Game, which was a scene I had been postponing and postponing. Somehow I felt the play couldn't exist without it. It had to be the Busby Berkeley part. I couldn't imagine how we were going to make seven gardeners, ten soldiers, ten courtiers, a king, a queen, a knave of hearts, tattling rose bushes, a croquet field, live hedgehog croquet balls, and live flamingo mallets, all out of six actors.

Saskia: We didn't start working on it until the last months before we opened at the Loft in New York. In the first improvisations, Larry was playing the King. We started with just Larry and me.

Andre: Saskia and Larry were doing improvisations in which she was trying to make him into the king she had always wanted. The man who would finally permit her to be a woman.

Saskia: My objective was to make him the most beautiful king, and his objective was to make me the most beautiful queen. You know, the things you most need out of each other. It was nice working with Larry. I understand his mind.

Andre: But the improvisations weren't getting anywhere. It was Saskia's thirtieth birthday and she was very upset about it. I knew how she felt, having just passed my thirty-fifth. There was a Grotowski benefit in New York which was limited to an audience of forty people, so it was practically impossible to get a ticket. I had one ticket. And I knew how important Grotowski was to Saskia. I'm really very selfish, but I finally decided to give her my ticket as a birthday present.

I wrapped it in tissue and put it in a large Japanese box lined in red velour. I watched her opening it. She couldn't tell what it was at first, because there was so much tissue and the box was so big. And then at last she found the ticket. She didn't say much, but I felt that suddenly she knew how much I cared about her.

Saskia: That same week I had just met someone and I was really in love with him. It was fantastic. I could just have closed the door and stayed for a week in bed with him. Everything was right.

Andre: The afternoon of my gift Saskia was like a savage in the improvisation. She was pained. She cried. She opened herself up. She really bared how much she needed a man to be her king. It was wonderful.

Saskia: I remember that rehearsal very well. The two of us had been playing games with each other, and it had been so nice that the games went out the window. There were moments when there were no games at all. And suddenly you knew how difficult it was to really be together. Just raw with each other. I remember that was a very full, very deep rehearsal for me.

Andre: I still had the idea that this scene had to be the extravaganza. I started looking for devices with the designer's help. Things like a change of lighting, party streamers, balloons released over the heads of the audience. But it all seemed too tricky. The actors had to do it themselves, the way they had in every other moment of the production.

Finally we were forced to come up with something for our first audience at the Loft. What the actors did was to turn the table from the Tea Party into a gate, swing it open and march into the garden. They got behind the table, sang one refrain from the "My Fair Lady Racing Song" and then froze while Tommy narrated the Croquet Game in the voice of this kind of Southern sports announcer. Then everybody started singing "De Camptown Races Sing Dis Song, Doo Dah," Tommy said, "They're off," and everybody started doing a sort of frenzied dance based on the head, chest, and shoulder details from the Plastiques, until one by one they exhausted themselves and disappeared behind the table. It was really vulgar.

Saskia: That scene developed much more fully after we started performing. We continued rehearsing while we played at the Loft in New York and at Cambridge.

Andre: When we got back to New York we still weren't happy with the Croquet Game. We'd been trying all sorts of other ways of dealing with it. One day Tommy walked in with this rubber mallet as a present for someone. It was all we needed. That day we chose the parts of the text we wanted, we did the balls, we did the wickets, everything. That rubber mallet was like the seed, and suddenly what we'd been struggling over for months was solved.

Saskia: When we put the play together we realized that it would have been very difficult for Larry to be the King, because right before that he has to be the Dormouse. The transition would have been too awkward. So Tommy became the King.

Tommy: My main objective as the King was to save Alice from getting her head bashed in by my lovely wife. That was another Lewis Carroll facet that I could connect with. A man who can only express himself through games. A weak figure in the presence of large, powerful women.

Saskia: The Red Queen is a very fast thinker. And to find herself always with these men around her—and none of them give her shit—enrages her. I think she has an ideal that somewhere she will be able to find fantastic men who will give her everything she wants. When she doesn't, she becomes furious.

Andre: The Croquet Game is the one time in the entire production where we use recorded music. It was Saskia's idea.

Saskia: The music in the Queen's Croquet Game is from *Jules et Jim.* I came to Andre and told him to use that music. The two of us went to a room and on an old record player we put the record. Now it goes better, but for a long time when I was alone with Andre I felt we were both very shy and didn't know how to be with each other, and so he sat down in the chair and fell over backward. It was a very awkward situation, but he heard the music and it immediately hit him as being right.

Andre: I felt it would help make the scene a kind of crescendo.

Saskia: So we played the music for the group. Someone said it was a typical German beer song. And they said, "Saskia is always trying to sell us on the Germans." They teased me. Friendly teasing, but it stung me. I was so angry I cried.

Andre: I think the other people in the company felt that it violated the restrictions we'd put on ourselves in the first half of the production, that in some way to use recorded music would infringe esthetically. But I really believe you have to permit yourself to break any rule in order to make something work. And the scene needed it.

Saskia: It upset me that they didn't listen to the music. That they didn't understand what that music is about. Because it is like the fullest joy with the fullest melancholy. And when they made fun of it, Andre said to me, "*Now* you say to them, 'Off with their heads.'"

You see, he was the only one, the only one, who understood.

THE RED QUEEN'S CROQUET

"Off with their heads!"

THE WHITE QUEEN

"The rule is . . . jam tomorrow and jam yesterday, but never, never jam today."

HUMPTY DUMPTY

"But let us suppose I were to . . . FALL."

Jerry: Andre predicted exactly what was going to happen with this show. He knew. He knew it was going to be a smash. Any guy who can do that I'll follow to the ends of the earth.

Larry: Andre kept saying—this is the way he inspires confidence—"People are probably not going to react very well to this, since it's our first work. So be prepared to fail." He kept saying that. But the work was so intense I don't think the question of success or failure came up too much. Then, when they did like it, it was fantastic.

Jerry: Andre treats each one of us differently.

Larry: He seems to be able to please everybody. He pleases me. I don't know how he does it. He's a magician.

Saskia: I think Andre's way of working is for the most part instinctive. That makes it very hard to believe in. People are not brought up to believe in that. The reason I stay with the group is that Andre is someone I can't get a grip on. I know it sounds infantile, but it's true. If I could read him like a book, I would quit. It's the surprises you give each other that I like so much. He's an enigma to me, and I think he knows it.

Andre: A lot of things in our work have come from accidents, but in a sense they are accidents we made happen. The forest of umbrellas was an accident. If it hadn't been raining the day we worked on that scene we probably would have made the forest some other way.

Larry: The forest of umbrellas came to me in a dream. Dreams are important in this kind of work. I dreamed feelings a lot. Dreamed fights between people. Making love to different people in the company. A lot of the feelings in the play came from dreams. Of course, I don't dream the way Andre does. Beautiful, lyrical, baroque things. I wish I did.

Tommy: I didn't have any dreams. I never do. And I don't believe Andre did either. He just pulled that dream about the Virgin Mary out of the air.

Andre: The forest is still an incomplete idea. One thing we have tried to do is to create, at each moment of the play, an emotional logic, even for the inanimate objects, which would then lead to the next stage of the journey. In that sense, the way the forest came into being was that when Alice hit the Red Queen, the men got so frightened that they grabbed the nearest thing, the umbrellas, to protect themselves. Having been scared by a woman, the next step is to get even with her, so they play a game in which, whenever the White Queen isn't looking, an umbrella tree begins sneaking up on her. It's a game I played as a kid, called Grandmother's Footsteps. If it's played right in the scene, the men can't possibly win, because the Queen is always moving. But the object is that if they are able to surround her they can end the scene that Saskia most wants to do in the whole play.

Saskia: The White Queen has a rhythm which we hardly ever use in our daily lives. For me she is almost an ideal person. She is intelligent and witty and likes to play games, but underneath all that is a big understanding. She knows that you can do anything with life. Whatever you want. Because who can tell you how to live? No one. Only yourself, your own heart, your own mind.

Andre: It is Saskia's most personal scene. She had a very strong feeling for the White Queen. She saw her as a woman living with a very special kind of freedom. The kind of woman I think Saskia would like to become.

Saskia: I remember one of the very first rehearsals for the White Queen. Larry and Andre were watching, and it was only Angela and me. I remember just where I was standing. I had the sheet, and Andre said, "Leap in," and I did. In that one rehearsal I found most of the things in the scene. They just came one right after the other. It was fantastic. Most things don't happen with that kind of ease.

Andre: In the other scenes we had begun by trying to find the action or impulse which could bring the word into being, as though we had never read it before. To do that we went through a lot of improvisations before we used the text. But for the White Queen and Humpty Dumpty and the White Knight—because they were all such personal scenes for the actors involved—we did very little improvisation outside the text. It was as though each actor took the words, dropped them down his well, and waited for the splash, the resonance.

Saskia: Bodily, I had the White Queen right away. But vocally it took me much longer. A phrase in Dutch like *Ik hou van je*—I love you—has many more associations in my mind than when I say, "I love you." My only association with "I love you" comes from the movies.

Andre: The only problem with the scene in rehearsals, and sometimes even now in performance, is that Saskia gets to feel it's too easy for her. It means so much to her that she occasionally distrusts the ease of it and tries to make it more difficult for herself.

Saskia: It is the most difficult scene for me. The White Queen is so relaxed and doesn't need to judge other people. She is just herself. She doesn't even question that, she just is.

Angela: In the beginning, when Saskia and I were doing the White Queen scene, it was very much a little Alice looking up at this wonderful woman whom she admired and hoped to become. And I looked for the things in Saskia that I admired and used those in the scene. But it was a little forced.

Saskia: At one point in the scene, the Queen says to Alice, "I daresay you haven't had much practice." For a long time that was very hard for me to say. It kept coming out like, "God damn it, do live backwards. You won't die. You won't lose your pots and your pans. But don't make it as if you can only live among pots and pans." It kept coming out angry. And that is not the White Queen.

Angela: I realize that the image I project to friends—I've been told this many times—is of a very meek, soft, fluffy, really dizzy little dum-dum. I guess it's conditioning. But I find that a lot of my strength is in lying low. It's all right if people think I'm dumb. They'll reveal more.

Saskia: Sometimes I get the feeling that Angela has been brought up to believe in this role-playing shit, but I question whether she's really happy in it. But who am I to say I know more about life than she does? But something in me says I do.

Angela: Saskia and I are really so different. I think in some way we both have this horrible feeling of superiority. Saskia appears to be so independent, and I admire that, but I often think in certain ways I'm freer than she is. I may be dependent on people but she's dependent on other things. Anyway, she's always questioning me, asking me what I think. Asking me some of the most personal questions. I love that about her. But I find I weigh what I say to her. I have the feeling that she's going to go home, put it all into a computer, and figure out something about me.

Saskia: Always searching: I'm sure Angela does that with me, too. I know she does. If the White Queen goes well, it is very different from all the other scenes as far as a relationship between two people is concerned. And I can get that from Angela because I'm a woman and I think she relaxes more.

Angela: The scene has really grown for me, so that now it is much more like two women confiding in each other, telling each other secrets that only women can share.

Saskia: Near the end of the scene, when I'm under the sheet, I give her a kind of little kick. I push her away. She's asking for the answers and I tell her there aren't any. I think it's frightening for her. It's very frightening when you suddenly see your mother doing something not as your mother, and you have suddenly to experience her as another person.

Andre: There's been a tremendous transformation in Saskia. A lot of it is physical. I don't notice this in anyone else, but sometimes when I'm sitting there watching the play I see her go through that same kind of change in the course of the performance. She passes through the Lory and this series of angry, emasculating women to the White Queen, and on certain nights when she has done the White Queen exquisitely well I can look at her while she's holding the ropes for Humpty Dumpty and it's incredible. It's as though she's been cleansed and purified and has turned into this exquisite sort of Vermeer girl. She looks totally at peace.

Jerry: My guess is that all of us, at one point or another, are playing a character very close to ourselves. Angela's a special case because she's got to be Alice, and Larry may be an exception, too, because I feel anything he does is very real to him. But for the rest of us, I believe there's one character we play who's really ourselves. I would be damned surprised if Saskia and the White Queen weren't a lot alike. I think Gerry is the White Knight. Tommy is definitely Lewis in that first scene. The crafty controller, that's Tommy all the way. And I'm Humpty Dumpty.

————————————

Andre: Jerry knew about Humpty Dumpty. Knew exactly what he wanted to say with the part. It was inside him. A lonely, isolated Beckett individual, stuck on top of a wall with no reason to live, and along comes a girl who is his last chance.

Jerry: About a month into the work on *Alice,* I took a real liking to Humpty Dumpty. I thought that it would be beautiful theater. He's sitting way up there and the girl is down on the floor: That physical relationship alone, together with the fact that in the end he falls and gets killed—well, you just can't miss.

Angela: Jerry Mayer is playing Humpty Dumpty because he has a very strong connection to that character. I see it in him constantly. Whenever a newcomer or a pretty girl comes into the room, there's a whole bon vivant mask Jerry puts on. It's precisely what Humpty does. It's painful to see because it's all a façade to hide his fragility. He's an orphan, and the group is his first real family.

Jerry: There was a time in my life when I used to tell girls about my background. They'd ask me something like, "Where are you from?" and I'd get into it. How when I was five my mother left me with my grandma who was a prostitute, and then I was put into a children's home and so on, you know, hitting the high spots. Some of it would be pretty humorous, because a lot of funny things did happen to me, but it would also be a little sad, because I would feel sad. I can really get into self-pity. And frequently I would find myself getting laid as a result of this story.

Angela: At first when Humpty starts to do all his great things, his imitations, his jokes, his whole song and dance, Alice is flattered that he's doing it for her. It looks as though she's going to have a good time with this guy.

103

Jerry: For me the greatest thing about the scene is the beginning, because she comes to me. I'm under the sheet, she pulls it off, and there we are. Sometimes I wish we could have stopped right there, because maybe, if I said or did the right thing, I could keep her.

Angela: I don't take him very seriously. He's making a great attempt to be charming and witty, but his puns aren't that clever and his jokes aren't that funny. I'm very gentle with him. I know he's fragile, so I can allow myself to appear inferior, sitting there nicely at his feet, shutting up when he tells me to. But it's not really all that nice. What she's really doing is not telling him where it's at. And why do you behave that way with someone? Because you don't want to get involved.

Andre: When Humpty starts talking about the White King—"all of his horses . . ."—Alice says, ". . . and all of his men, yeah." She knows that poem. She knows what's going to happen to him, that he's going to fall off the wall and break.

Angela: Who wants to get involved with a loser? There's something old about Humpty. I don't know what it is. Maybe it's because I know he's going to die. But I see him as an old man. There's that little movement he makes, it's almost like someone in a wheelchair. And I humor him because it's sort of touching to see this old man making a great attempt to win me over.

Jerry: Humpty is very much the kind of a guy who can cut his own throat with his mouth. And even while he's cutting his throat and knows it—this is so much like me—he's enjoying his bon mot and congratulating himself for some verbal flourish. When Alice says she's seven and a half and he makes his little joke about it—"My advice would have been to leave off at seven"—I think that probably puts her off, but I can't help it, I really enjoy saying it.

Angela: I know Humpty needs me to be there and to be his audience, but I don't laugh. You think I don't get that joke? I get it. An idiot would get that joke. I just don't laugh. That's a willful, hostile choice on my part.

Jerry: I know what those jokes are about. I make jokes like that all the time. You see, it's really very hard for me to say I want something. So I phrase it as a joke, which makes it sound as though it doesn't matter to me.

Angela: I really would like to be Jerry's friend. But I don't think he'll ever let me get close enough to him to be hurt by me. And I don't even know that I want to take the responsibility, or even be bothered.

Jerry: What has to happen in Humpty Dumpty for it to go well is for me to really need her. I have to come out to that little girl and try to touch her. And that's very much Angela for me. I don't relate to her much as Alice. Hell, I don't know what Alice is. But I relate to her a lot as Angela.

Angela: I feel guilty about Jerry. Socially I think I've had almost everybody over to dinner. And I've never invited Jerry. Maybe because he's alone. Which is really all the more reason to do it. But I never have.

Jerry: I really love Angela. In a very solid way. Not that I would ever go so far as to try and make her mine—although who can say. But I have often thought that it's a good thing our scene is staged the way it is with me way up there on the chairs and her down on the floor. Because I can see how the whole thing could have become a lot more sexual. But this way I can't reach her, I can't physically get hold of her, except maybe to touch her hand. But I guess it intensifies the feeling Andre wanted: that the whole thing is really impossible.

Angela: I can't separate Jerry from Humpty. My feelings in the scene are all mixed up with my feelings for Jerry. I would like Jerry to trust me and consider me his friend, but I think I often push him away, merely by my passivity toward his problems. Because I feel incapable of dealing with them. People like that, who are so negative, scare me.

Jerry: There's another thing about me that has a lot to do with Humpty. I often find myself more drawn to the women I can't reach than to those I can.

Angela: When Humpty is about to recite this poem for me, I definitely don't want to listen. I even say so. He tells Alice, "I can recite poetry as well as the next fellow when it comes to that," and her answer is, "It needn't come to that." Seems to me that's a pretty blunt way of saying, Don't do it. But he goes right ahead.

Andre: I don't know how Jerry feels about the poem. For me its meaning has always been perfectly clear. It's about the desire to murder your brothers and the terror of the intensity of that desire to kill. "I sent a message to the fish, I told them, 'This is what I wish. . . .' The little fishes' answer was, 'We cannot do it, Sir, because. . . .'" They can't get out of your life, they can't die, because they don't want to. "I sent to them again to say, 'It would be better to obey.'" You keep warning them, but they refuse to take heed. So, "I took that corkscrew from the shelf"—there's a marvelous twisted gesture Jerry makes as he's going for the corkscrew—"and went to do the deed myself." It's so obvious. "When I found the door was shut I tried to turn the handle but. . . ." Because there is that locked door in yourself that won't permit you to kill your brothers. So, in the face of that terrible frustration, you kill yourself.

Jerry: I have never understood why that poem works. What I'm doing when I recite that poem is trying to create a mood, an emotion, through sound. Because the words of the poem aren't very sensible. I mean, I'll be damned if I know what that poem means.

Andre: There is something about the sound of Humpty's poem. For me it has to sound like autumn. As soon as he says, "In autumn when the leaves are brown, take pen and ink and write it down," if it doesn't have that crisp, autumnal sound, like a church bell ringing in the country, I know it won't get personal.

Angela: That poem means nothing to Jerry? I won't believe he hasn't made that poem very personal to him. Maybe I'm too sentimental, but I see it as his whole journey through life to where he is now as an adult. That he was very open as a young kid and then he went from one foster home to another, like in the poem he says, "I found the door was shut." And he fought for a while, but now I don't think he fights anymore. The killing he did was something in himself.

Jerry: I never know until she goes whether I've won or lost. And there are times when I can see she really doesn't want to leave. I know she has to, because it's there in the blocking. Part of me knows that. But if I can see she doesn't want to go, that's very strong for me.

Angela: Andre has told Jerry he should drive me away with his last lines. But I don't feel driven away. I look for my out and I go. I know when I turn away from him that Humpty ain't gonna come to no good sitting on top of those chairs, waiting for somebody to come by and save him. The same way I know Jerry ain't gonna come to no good in that little apartment watching his TV all by himself day and night.

Andre: The splattering of the egg in Humpty's suicide was my idea. I remember suggesting that to Jerry. Originally he had thought of playing the scene with a hardboiled egg so there would be no danger.

Jerry: I thought of breaking the egg over my heart, but I decided that was probably too corny.

Andre: One day I said to Jerry, "Don't you think it would be great when you commit suicide to break the egg on your face?" I don't think he liked it much at first, but the minute he saw what it did to an audience he loved it.

Jerry: When I throw myself off the chairs, I suppose maybe a lot of people think of that as a suicide. I don't. You can't kill yourself by breaking an egg on your head and falling off a stack of chairs. But there's one thing about that fall. In order to do it right—it may look hard but it's really not— the movement I make has to be very sharp, like a hand clap. When I make that movement, if I do it right, there's only one feeling it can bring up in me and that is anger. In that respect, I guess you could say it's a suicide.

_____

Angela: Somewhere in the book it says that when Alice would recall all her experiences in Wonderland, the White Knight would be the person she would remember most vividly with a mixture of bittersweet feelings. Gerry Bamman and I set up these improvisations that definitely were not childlike. We were trying to find a way of getting at the intimate feelings between the Knight and Alice that we felt were suggested in the book.

Gerry: We began realistically with the White Knight. Thinking about him as old, since he is, in the book. Using a table for his horse. A real box. A real sword. A real fight with another knight. But as we went through it, one thing began impressing itself on me, namely, that most of the things he says are really very ungentle, contrary to the way he's pictured in the Tenniel drawings, as this sweet, fragile old man. Nor is Alice sweet with him. We tried working on that aspect—a relationship between the two of them that would comprehend those feelings. We put it in a lot of different contexts. Mother and son. Teacher and student.

Angela: Then we tried building the relationship of a man and a woman who had been living together. The moment when both realize the relationship is going nowhere because the man is determined to go on playing games and the woman needs more.

Gerry: The more we made the objects unrealistic, figments of the Knight's mind, the more sense it began to make to us. If he said something about a box, it wasn't necessarily because there was a box there. It was because he saw a box. If he said something about a horse, it didn't necessarily mean there was a horse there. He just saw one. It was obvious to me that he must be seeing things other people weren't seeing. Anybody who puts anklets around his horse's legs to keep the sharks away is afraid of something that other people aren't afraid of.

Then one day we felt he seemed like a speed freak, seeing all these things that were invisible to everybody else. It triggered something for me. It didn't have much to do with drugs, and certainly doesn't now. But the frenzy of that improvisation felt accurate to me. That's when we took it to Andre and began working with him.

Andre: Gerry never discussed his concept of the White Knight with me. It is his most personal scene and the most personal one for me as well. I think both of us were reluctant to articulate our feelings about it, as though we believed that that would harm it. We were very close in our understanding of that character. And even now when I give notes and I feel the scene has slipped a little, all I say is, "He wasn't really there tonight." Or, "The chain was broken." The three of us understand.

Gerry: Once we reached that moment in the speed freak improvisation which set up reverberations in all of us—Angela, Andre, and me—there was no more technique involved. It's the only time I have reached that level. In anything I've done.

There were no longer any familiar actor's tools. There was something else there. I still can't explain it, but once the scene begins it propels you forward.

All I can say is that a good many of the things that happen in that scene are built on a pain in the middle part of my body, right around my solar plexis. A real physical pain that grips me every time I'm in a situation like that: ending a relationship with a girl, or not even necessarily ending it but dealing with the most personal sexual aspects of that relationship in an unfriendly way. For me it's like a knife in the gut. It's a pain so frightening that I would do almost anything to avoid it. Which only makes it all the more intense.

Angela: When you have a desperate need to say something to someone close to you, but for some damn reason you can't put it into words, what usually happens — at least to me — is that it grows and grows and then it comes bursting out, but never the way you wanted. It gets all turned around and you end up hurting that person.

Gerry: There's a point just before each of those games, each of those tirades, when something in you says, I can't do that, I can't hurt that person. But finally you do. And once you've begun it's so easy, incredibly easy, you can't stop. From the beginning of that scene I know that I'm going to leave. That I have to. And yet I also have to stay. Those two things are what have always been the tensions in the scene: things pulling you both ways until you're strung out like a spring at its limit.

Andre: Alice may be in an impossible situation with the White Knight. If she refuses to play along with his fantasies, she drives him into a rage against her and against himself. If she does play along with him she becomes an accomplice, nurturing the very thing in him that is destroying them both.

Angela: So when I say, right at the beginning, "I don't want to be anybody's prisoner. I want to be a queen," it has special implications for me: I'm not going to put on the mask he wants me to wear so that he will love me. I don't want to be a toy. I want to be a woman.

Gerry: It seems to me that she wants to talk about the situation, and that's the last thing the Knight wants to do. The last thing he wants to do is to sit down and have a long heart-to-heart talk about their past relationship and what the dismal future holds.

Angela: I'm trying to get him to communicate with me without the games. But no matter what I do he won't let up. He's not talking about us. He's talking about puddings and horses that aren't there. When I reach out to touch him, he pushes me away. And when I want him to hold me, he throws me over his shoulder.

Andre: But what does she really offer him as an alternative? She says no a lot. When he talks about his imaginary pudding she tells him it doesn't sound very nice, and when he demonstrates one of his inventions she tells him it's impossible. But what does she give him instead? She doesn't give him sex. She doesn't really offer herself as a woman. She just says no.

Gerry: There are lots of things we're saying to each other under the lines—things which came out in improvisations. Alice accuses me of being insane and I say, "If you think I'm insane now you haven't seen anything yet." She says, "You're hurting me." And I say, "Yes, I'm hurting you, and you haven't been hurt enough yet." Because I had to make her keep playing and responding. She couldn't brush me off and get out of it that easily.

Angela: I guess I don't really want to get out of it. In all my relationships, regardless of how painful they may be, I don't like to be the one who leaves. I refuse to walk out. Maybe I don't want to take the responsibility for ending it, or maybe I always believe I can salvage something. But what often happens in those situations is that they get dragged out and become unbearable.

Gerry: I wish I could have what the old man has in the Knight's song: clear eyes, white hair, and a gentle voice. A kind of peace. But it's just not possible. It is possible to get a kind of peace, but it is one that can only lead to disturbance.

Angela: Gerry's not the only one who inflicts suffering in that scene. I know my tears affect him, and I'm definitely in control of my tears. I mean Alice is. She's hurting him and she knows it. He may be getting pleasure out of it too, because there is something in Gerry that likes to see women cry. Otherwise he wouldn't have walked out so often on so many women. But I admit I do make him suffer in that scene.

Gerry: One of the things that always has torn me apart, and still does, is that there are moments when there is a temptation to stop and remain. There are moments when she is saying, "Please talk to me," and his answer is, "I am talking to you in the only way I know how." Because there is a part of him that wants to communicate with her, wants to be able not to play. But he cannot, I cannot, change. And I know it. I know that nothing either of us can do will make this work. That is the process the scene embodies for me; wanting an unattainable object, knowing it is unattainable but continuing to pursue it.

Angela: Regardless of what Alice says, she's really not prepared to leave the White Knight. She enjoys suffering with him. She puts up with it and loves him for it. In the end, she embraces him right in the middle of this whole, stupid, endless song. At that point she doesn't care any more. If he'll just hold her and rock her, she'll stay and he can do anything he wants with her. And what he does at last is leave. But even as he's leaving, all she can say is, "I liked the song." She repeats it over and over. She doesn't give a damn about her terms any more. All she wants is for him to stay. But he can't.

Gerry: There are people who hate the play. And hate the White Knight in particular. People have come to me and said they didn't understand it because I talked too fast. I can only reply that it's irrelevant to me. I can see how it can be very relevant to them and how irritating it can be for them. But I am no more interested in being understood verbally than I would be if I were driving my cab and somebody smashed into me and I started screaming at him. And I don't think he would need to hear all my words in order to understand what I was trying to communicate.

Andre: The only way the scene can go well is if Angela and Gerry have a total sense of privacy while they're doing it. If they feel pressured to get through it for the sake of the audience, because the audience is often exhausted at this point, then the moments between Gerry and Angela become empty and the scene seems to go more slowly. They must have the nerve to hold each moment, each demand, each protest to the breaking point. Then the rhythm builds and the scene seems to go faster.

Gerry: We did what we had to do. We did not construct the play for an audience. I suppose, from some audiences' reactions, that if we were trying to make a well-made piece it would have to end with the Tea Party. But we couldn't have done it that way.

Andre: One mysterious and marvelous thing, because it is unconscious, is that we should begin and end the play with two scenes that are so similar, almost like fun-house mirror images of each other. It was not something I had planned on or even thought about.

Gerry: It's as natural for us to do that as it is for an object thrown into the air to fall to the ground. The most exciting thing is probably its ascent, but it would be incomplete if it didn't land anywhere. The play reaches its peak in the Tea Party. But what goes up must come down. And it does. And it is the only way that the experience can be complete for us.

THE WHITE KNIGHT

"I weep
for it reminds me so
of that old man
I used to know . . .
Whose look was mild,
Whose speech was slow,
Whose hair
was whiter than the snow,
With eyes like cinders
all aglow,
Who seemed distracted
with his woe . . ."

Gerry: We had no idea what it was we had. As far as we could guess, we had a black tragedy on our hands. It certainly wasn't funny. Not to us. Nothing we had done had anything to do with getting a laugh.

Larry: We weren't at all ready for New Jersey, but they had offered us twenty-five dollars each for a performance. We were all broke and we really needed the money.

Gerry: So we got to that first performance in New Jersey, and the house was torn apart with laughter.

Larry: They'll never be another audience like that. It was out of sight. The play was still rough. We had no ending for certain scenes. In fact, we hadn't figured out an ending for the whole play, so we just had to walk off stage. They absolutely flipped out!

Gerry: ·The reaction really threw us. And for me it was especially so in the White Knight scene. I went off after that performance and they were applauding and they loved it and I said, "They can't thank me enough for the two years I've put into this."

Larry: Afterward we stayed around so we could talk with the audience. They just sat and stared at us like we were a miracle. One girl said to Gerry Bamman, "I thought you were the essence of man." Somebody said to me, "Wow, are you always that high?" We were in shock. We had no idea the play could get a response like that. We'd been off in some tunnel for two years.

After New Jersey we took *Alice* around to the Loft in New York, and then up to Syracuse. People were really excited. We were getting fantastic responses the whole time. When we got back and opened at the Extension, the reviews were great, and a different group of people started coming. We all began losing interest because the audiences weren't as wild as they had been at first.

Gerry: After a year of performances it starts to change. You start doing things to please the audience. It's a real danger. You've got to keep doing it for yourselves.

Larry: We had to start reexamining where we were at. The great audiences had been terrific, but because of them, because of the surprise of it all, we had started directing all our energies toward the audience, to get their response, instead of directing our energies toward each other and letting the audiences watch what was happening. That was the secret, the real secret of what we had done.

Saskia: I sometimes get angry at the audience. Especially the ones that laugh all the time and applaud everything. It makes me feel that they only catch on to what's obvious. They become for me a bunch of sheep. Laugh silly, you know: "Haw, haw, haw!" When you've worked on something very hard you don't want people to respond so easily.

Andre: The actor is always aware of the audience no matter how concentrated, no matter how involved he is. And God knows this is a concentrated group of actors. They know everyone in that audience.

Tommy: I can't help but be aware of the audience, especially when they laugh. But all the other actors will say to me, "Did you see that guy?" I don't understand how they do it, mainly because without my glasses, I'm blind. I do wear one contact lens. A man was making me up a set but he died and only one was finished. Since then I've never had the money to get a full set, so I get by with one. So if I can just see the other actors I'm overjoyed. I never see the audience.

Andre: The actors don't need the audience to play. But the audience completely changes the event. I suppose that sounds illogical but it's true. In some strange, delicate way they're part of the performance.

It's almost as if there's a second audience. There's the audience for the play and there's the audience for the total event. It's like somebody's watching us all. That's like the actor's own audience. I think each of us is playing for someone. Each of us has someone he's giving this gift to.

Angela: When you have an audience that responds, it spurs you on. It moves you to do more. I feel we're giving them a gift. They might not like it, but it's still a gift. It's so personal and we're letting them watch. It took me three years with this group to get to the point where I could let down my defenses, and now I'm letting the audience watch me, too. Watch me being foolish or clumsy. I can't think about it or I couldn't do the show.

Larry: It's hard with a stiff audience. You have to go into each other more.

Angela: You have to shut them out. But Tommy's there. Larry's there. My friends are there.

Larry: Sometimes I literally have to say to myself, "I'm here playing a game with my friends. I've got to play and I've got to have fun doing it." Now what is it about Angela that makes me want to do these things to her? Sometimes during the performance I say out loud, "Why? Why?" So I can find the answer.

Andre: When we performed *Alice* in the Berkshires, we played outdoors, in the woods, which seemed to everybody a beautiful idea. We set up some seats and put the parachute up overhead, and because it was grassy and a little uneven we built a platform for the actors. It was maybe two inches high. That destroyed the event: it created a barrier between the actors and the audience that seemed like miles. Suddenly it was a theater.

Angela: Grotowski's people warm up before every performance, and it seems like they really break their backs. Andre comes in with us an hour and a half before the show and we warm up. Some of us sit and talk to him, talk to each other, tell stories. There are some nights when I may just do one little headstand. Or while I'm putting my costume on I'll run my voice up the scales. I've come to realize that Andre's warm-up is simply being together. That's the important part. Being together.

Tommy: The magnificent thing about our group is that we have built an actor-owned company. That's a real feat. There hasn't been an actor-owned company since the eighteenth century, I think. We're a non-profit corporation. We are the board of directors. We pay ourselves. We know where the money goes. And we know that none of us are going to be fired tomorrow. That gives us an incredible sense of security that can't possibly exist in any other company.

Gerry: We haven't faded into each other. The only thing that prevented that was Andre's way of work. The fact that he approached us daily with no preconceptions and let each of us make our own discoveries. So our own persons become vital to the work process, whereas in most ensembles they are merely tools for a uniform result.

Saskia: Most directors impose themselves on their actors and the actors come out all the same as if there is some kind of glue over them.

Larry: And we respect each other. Not so much for our abilities. There are still people in the group I don't think can act for beans. And I'm sure other people feel the same way. But we have a certain kind of respect for the fact that we have all lived through this together.

Tommy: We've gone beyond friendships. At one point or another I've hated everyone. The first thing you learn is to be easy with one another. Then you learn not to be easy with one another.

Larry: I suppose if I didn't work with these people I'd never see them. We don't socialize together much. Other groups are much more involved with each other. They have to love each other, because in the work they feel each other up. Suck each other's feet. The thought of sucking Gerry Bamman's foot is so repulsive to me. I mean I don't love him. Not that way.

Andre: The performance is everything. Because *Alice in Wonderland* is like a trampoline for the life of the group. On an ideal night the audience should be able to see everything we went through together in those two years. That's why I have to be there every night. I'm part of the performance. At least they believe I am, and I believe I am, which makes it true.

Saskia: When you do a hundred performances of *Alice,* you try to find each night the life, the interaction, the being together. But of course some nights you can't find it, and on those nights, the pleasing things come in. You start doing it for Andre, and if he's not there it really makes a difference.

Larry: Because everything we do is done for him, I suppose. He was our only audience for such a long time. And when he's not there watching the play, it seems like something's missing.

Saskia: He went away for six weeks a while ago and I was amazed at my reaction. Nobody saw it but I almost cried. Then, after two performances with him not there, I got past it. The red light came on and I started to watch myself about it.

Angela: I think my feelings of insecurity are greatest now. You secretly expect everything to change when you get what you've been striving for your whole adult life. I always knew that what I wanted from my profession was to be able to respect myself, not just be somebody's pawn. Now I've gotten that. And somehow, when your dream comes true, you start to feel, This is it? This is all there is?

Andre: I wish the audience for *Alice* could be limited to those people who sit on the floor. That way there is no separation between them and the actors. They share one world. Those who sit on the floor become like children. The actors seem bigger than they are. Also, they're right under the parachute, so that they and the actors are joined. I think the theater is like a church. There's a place for the priest and a place for the congregation. Each knows his boundaries, and yet they are somehow unified. They can't exist without one another.

There are certain moments in *Alice* when an actor is about three inches away from your face. You can smell him. You can reach out and touch him if you want — you do have that right — there he is — and he can touch you. But you don't. Yet each of you knows it's possible. And feels that it's possible. And that is tense. That is exciting.

There are two realities in the theater. The audience *is,* and the actor acts at being. Once you touch you've violated the magical joining of those two realities and you expose that it is unreal.

THE
BACKWARDS
FALL

''Down, down, down,
me with here down were
you wish I dear
my Dinah . . .''

118

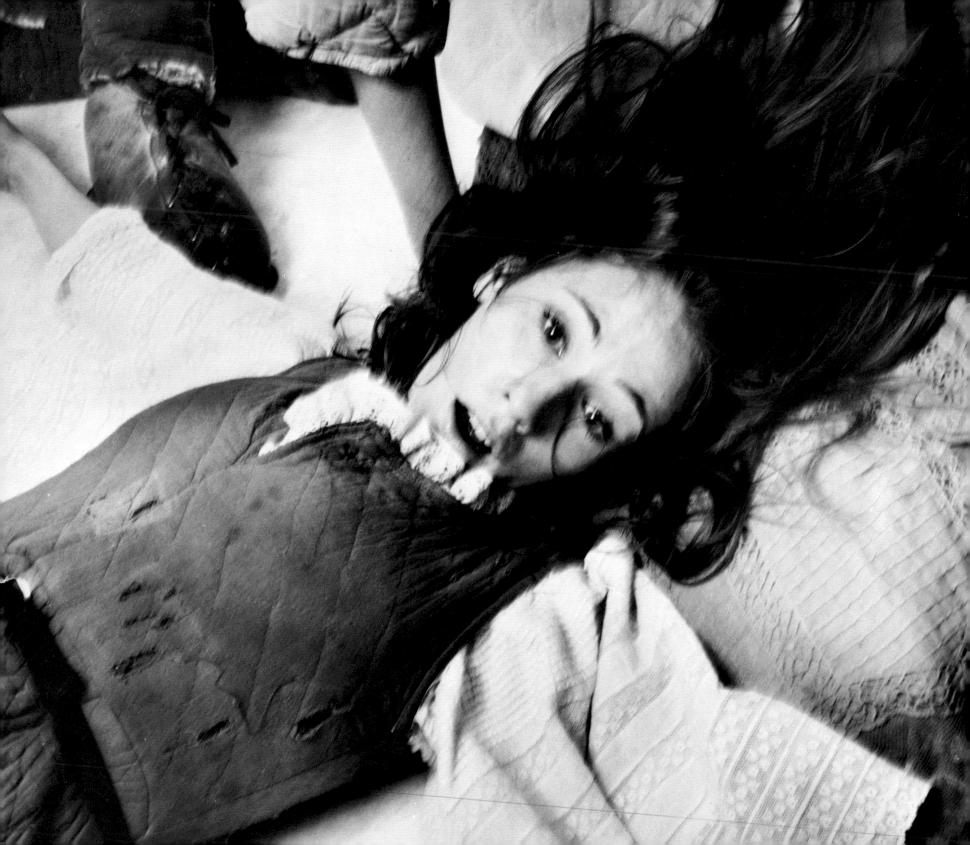

Larry: About once every three weeks
I lose what I'm doing. I have to go
to Andre and say, "Andre, I've
lost it." And he puts me back on it.
Always does.
Because he knows what it's all about.
See, I don't know what this play is.
I've never seen it. None
of us has.

THE END

The Play

THE CAST /

GERRY BAMMAN / Part of The Jabberwocky Monster
White Rabbit
A Shelf in The Fall
Glass Table
Key to The Little Door
Mouse
Caterpillar's Hookah
Singing Mushroom
Frog Footman
March Hare
Red Queen's Gardener
Croquet Ball
Weeping Willow Tree in the Forest
Wall of the Sheep's Shop
First King's Man
White Knight

TOM COSTELLO / Part of The Jabberwocky Monster
Rabbit Maker
Vertigo
Lewis Carroll
Dirigible Prince
The Little Door
Glass Table Leg
Garden
Agent
Sea Serpent
Buoy in the Pool of Tears
Dodo
Hunchback of Notre Dame Monster
Wall of the Neat Little House
Singing Mushroom
Cheshire Cat
King of Hearts
Croquet Stake
Spreading Chestnut Tree in the Forest
Wall of Sheep's Shop
Second King's Man
First Gravedigger

SASKIA NOORDHOEK HEGT / Part of The Jabberwocky Monster
Sister Liddell
Vertigo
Water Spirit in the Pool of Tears
Lory
Red Cat Monster
Wall of the Neat Little House
Singing Mushroom
Duchess
Queen of Hearts
White Queen
Fortune Telling Sheep
King's Man
Weeping Widow

JERRY MAYER / Part of The Jabberwocky Monster
Dodgson The Storyteller
Fog Horn in the Pool of Tears
Grandfather Crab
Front Door of the Neat Little House
Singing Mushroom
Voice of the Duchess' Baby
Mad Hatter
Red Queen's Gardener
Croquet Ball
Oak Tree in the Forest
Wall of Sheep's Shop
Humpty Dumpty

ANGELA PIETROPINTO / Alice

LARRY PINE / Part of The Jabberwocky Monster
Rabbit's Heartbeat
Hole
Vertigo
Water Spirit in the Pool of Tears
Duck
Executioner's Victim Monster
Roof of the Neat Little House
Fire that burns down the Neat Little House
Caterpillar
Duchess' Cook
Dormouse
Red Queen's Gardener
White King's Snore
Pine Tree in the Forest
Bird in the Forest
Wind in the Forest
Wall of the Sheep's Shop
King's Man
Second Gravedigger

The audience enters a room made entirely of real, old doors—doors you might find in a deserted tenement or surrounding a construction site. The feeling is of a secret clubhouse perhaps, a room completely closed in by doors. In this room are a large, old-fashioned scale on which you can weigh yourself; a 1920s radio over which comes music from Bons Bons aus Wein; and a table with cookies and lemonade. Scrawled in chalk on the doors, pointing to the free cookies and lemonade, are signs which say: EAT ME and DRINK ME. The audience waits or plays, not knowing where to go next. Just as the performance is about to begin, a very small door, three feet high, opens, and the audience crawls through into the environment, to the music of The Sheik of Araby, which is playing over an old victrola. The moment the audience is seated the lights go out, and the Jabberwocky Monster breaks through the paper curtain.

The manxome foe he sought.

JERRY: 'Twas brillig and the slithy toves did gyre and gimble in the wabe; all mimsy were the borogroves, and the mome raths outgrabe . . .

LARRY: Beware the jabberwock, my son. The jaws that bite, the claws that catch; beware the jubjub bird, and shun the frumious bandersnatch. . . .

ANGELA: He took his vorpal sword in hand, long time. . . .

ALL: Looooooong time.

ANGELA: The manxome foe he sought. So rested he by a tumtum tree, and stood awhile in thought. *(Attempting to break out of center.)*

SASKIA: And as in uffish thought he stood, the Jabberwock with eyes of flame, came whiffling through the tulgey wood, and burbled as it came.

GERRY: One, two. One, two. And through and through the vorpal blade went snicker-snack. He left it dead and with its head, he went galumphing back.

TOM: And hast thou slain the jabberwock? Come to my arms, my beamish boy! O frabjous day! Callooh! Callay! He chortled in his joy.

JERRY: *(As Jerry repeats his verse, the others say their own verse.)* 'Twas brillig, and the slithy toves did gyre and gimble in the wabe: all mimsy were the borogroves, and the mome raths outgrabe. *(All fall apart. Larry begins rowing. Jerry gets stool and sits. Saskia and Angela cross and form tableau as Alice and her sister sitting by the bank. Saskia reads as Alice daydreams with her head in her sister's lap.)*

JERRY/DODGSON: All in a golden afternoon, full leisurely we glide; for both our oars with little hands are plied. . . . *(Stops, thinks.)* for both our oars are plied . . . *(Thinks.)* . . . All in a golden afternoon, full leisurely we glide; for both our oars by little . . . *(Gives up.)*

All in a golden afternoon . . .

LARRY: *(Rowing becomes more and more desperate, suddenly stops, throws down oar.)* Alice! A childish story take and with a gentle hand lay it, where childhood dreams are twined in memory's mystic band . . . like a pilgrim's withered wreath of flowers plucked in a far-off land. *(He begins to make heart beats by beating with his fists on the floor. Tom forms Gerry into white rabbit and at the final moment of creation the rabbit screams. Alice sees the rabbit and Larry creates a hole with his body for the rabbit to escape into. Alice follows, and just as she enters the hole they all freeze.)*

DODGSON: Alice! . . . And her sister, sitting on the bank, beginning to get rather tired, with the hot day, and considering, in her own mind . . . when suddenly a white rabbit with pink eyes ran right by her. In another moment, down went Alice after it. *(The fall begins—a series of swings, throws and catches of Alice by the other actors, much like children's games. After the initial scream the fall is done silently while Dodgson continues.)* Well, after such a fall as this, I shall think nothing of falling downstairs . . . how brave they'll all think me at home . . . down, down, down . . . would the fall never come to an end? I wonder if I shall fall right through the Earth . . . how curious that would be . . . down, down, down. . . . Dinah, my dear, I wish you were down here with me but there are no mice in the air, but you might catch a bat, and that's very like a mouse, you know, but do cats eat bats, I wonder, do cats eat bats . . . do bats eat cats . . . when suddenly thump! Thump! Down she came on a bed of sticks and dry leaves and the fall was over. *(This speech and the children's swinging games end simultaneously and all the actors except Dodgson fall to the ground and lie still for a moment until next burst of energy.)*

. . . down, down, down . . .

ALL: *(To Alice as they scurry around her.)* Oh my ears and whiskers! Oh my ears and whiskers. *(All go under table, leaving only Alice and Lewis.)*

ALICE: Oh my ears and whiskers!

LEWIS: *(Screams.)* We are in a long dark hall; there are doors all around the hall and all of them are locked! *(Jerry laughs mysteriously from under the table.)* We proceed down the hall. *(Lewis pulls Alice to her feet.)*

ALICE: We do?

LEWIS: We do. You first. *(Pushes her down front. Gerry screams from under table.)*

ALICE: What was that? *(She crouches down with her hair hanging down in front of her face.)*

LEWIS: Wait . . . right in front of you there is a beautiful, golden curtain . . . and behind that curtain there is . . .

Oh my ears and whiskers!

ALICE: *(Parting her hair away from her face.)*
The Rabbit!

LEWIS: A door! *(Making himself into a door.)*

(Together.)

ALICE: A door? ... Oh, the door. He had to get out of here someway. *(She tries to open the door.)*

LEWIS: But you are in the mysterious hall of Locked Doors! *(Jerry's mysterious laugh.)*

ALICE: We need a key.

LEWIS: Don't look now, but right behind you there is a little glass table, and on that table there is a tiny golden K-E-Y. Don't look. Reach back and get the key. *(Gerry has crept out from under the table and snuck up behind Alice and becomes the table. Alice reaches back and touches his head.)*

ALICE: It's fuzzy!

LEWIS: Get the key! *(She does and opens the door.)*

ALICE: *(As she pushes the door/Lewis open.)* It works! *(Music: all but Alice: "Stars and Stripes Forever March.")* No, no, no. It's a garden *(Lewis cuts the music.)* ... it's a garden ... you know ... with trees and flowers and fountains. *(All but Alice make garden sounds—birds chirping and water splashing—and Jerry sings "Spring Song.")* Oh, yes ... and birds ... I love birds ... oh, could we ... come on, let's go. *(Alice tries to push her way through but Lewis sits up, pushing her back and thereby closing the door to the garden.)*

LEWIS: No! You're too big.

ALICE: We've got to make that door bigger.

LEWIS: No, we've got to make you smaller.

ALICE: Yeah! How are we going to do that?

LEWIS: It's easy. You get bigger every day ... right?

ALICE: Right.

LEWIS: How do you do that?

ALICE: Naturally.

LEWIS: Yes, but by ...

ALICE: Eating.

LEWIS: And what's the opposite of eating?

We are in a long dark hall.

ALICE: Not eating.

LEWIS: No. The opposite of eating is . . . dddddd.

ALICE: That's it . . . you've got it . . . give me a hint.

LEWIS: I am giving you a hint. D.d.d.d.d.d. . . .

ALICE: It begins with a d.d.d.d.? Eating. . . . Drinking. . . . Drinking?

LEWIS: Yes.

ALICE: Yes? I got that the first guess.

LEWIS: Don't look now, but you know that little glass table where you found the k-e-y? Well, on that little table there is a small glass bottle, and on that bottle are written the magic words

JERRY. Drink Me. *(Alice turns to see.)*

LEWIS: Don't look!

ALICE: No . . . I wouldn't look.

LEWIS: Go and get that bottle and bring it here to me.

ALICE: Get the bottle.

LEWIS: And bring it to me.

ALICE: Stay. *(Alice goes and picks up the bottle.)*

JERRY: *(Whisper.)* Drink me. *(Alice does drink.)*

LEWIS: Alice! Bring me that bottle.

ALICE: I drank it all . . . oh, I drank it all.

LEWIS: You drank that awfully fast, didn't you?

ALICE: Yes. It was piggy of me.

LEWIS: What did it taste like?

ALICE: Cherry tarts . . . hot buttered toast . . . roast turkey. . . .

LEWIS: Mmmmmm . . . turkey.

ALICE: Pineapple.

LEWIS: Pineapple . . . ?

ALICE: Custard.

I am giving you a hint. D.d.d.d. . . .

LEWIS: Custard . . . I knew it. Do you know what else tastes like custard?

ALICE: No, no . . . what else?

LEWIS: Arsenic!

ALICE: Arsen . . . that's a poi . . .

LEWIS: Poison! *(Alice collapses in his arms.)* . . . However, just because it tasted like poison . . .

ALICE: I've been poisoned . . . I'm going *(She puts one leg into his arms.)* . . . I'm going beautifully.*(The other leg goes up so that he is holding her in his arms.)*

. . . I'm going beautifully . . .

LEWIS: . . . is no reason to believe . . . Alice! . . . Alice . . .

ALICE: I did it for you. . . . I did it because I love you . . . *(Kisses him.)*

LEWIS: Alice! You're getting smaller . . . and smaller . . . and smaller . . . *(Puts her down.)*

ALICE: That's what we wanted to do. Oh, look at my little hands.

LEWIS: . . . and smaller . . . *(As he pushes her down into crouching position.)* . . . just like a beautiful . . . little . . . bug.

ALICE: No, but look at my little eyes . . . my little nose . . .

You're getting smaller . . . and smaller . . .

LEWIS: Proboscis.

ALICE: Those little lips . . . *(She takes his hand and kisses it.)* . . . giving you little kisses, right from my little heart . . . just like a little doll.

LEWIS: Doll?

ALICE: Doll.

LEWIS: All right. Doll.

ALICE: And that little doll can go right into the garden.

LEWIS: No, she can't.

ALICE: Why not?

LEWIS: Because you are in the mysterious hall of Locked Doors. *(Jerry's mysterious laugh.)*

ALICE: But I have the key.

LEWIS: Where, little doll?

ALICE: I put the key . . . on the table when I went to get the bottle.

LEWIS: On the table, little doll? . . . On the table that now rises fifty feet of sheer

. . . look at my little eyes, my little nose . . .

130

glass, straight up *(Points with straight arm up to table towering above them.)* . . . I can almost see the little key . . . way up there.

ALICE: Oh yeah. I can see it . . . so you mustn't get upset.

LEWIS: I'm not upset.

ALICE: I'll go right up the leg. *(Uses Lewis as the leg and tries to climb up him.)* Stay still. These glass legs are very slippery, you know.

LEWIS: Cake! . . . Cake . . . *(He starts to put her down.)*

ALICE: Wait, I've almost got . . . no, don't put me down . . . you're . . .

LEWIS: *(Puts her on the ground.)* FREEZE! *(She is silenced.)* . . . Because just before you fell, I saw this magnificent chocolate layer cake with fudge frosting . . . and written on top in singing mushrooms were the magic words:

GERRY: Eat me.

ALICE: Where is this cake?

LEWIS: Get up very carefully, and it won't even be squashed . . . hoop-la.

ALICE: Squashed? *(Looks under her dress.)* No wait. Let me think. If I eat the cake . . . I'll get bigger and I can get the key.

LEWIS: *(Offering his hands to help her up.)* Right. Hoop-la.

ALICE: But if I eat the cake and I get smaller?

LEWIS: Then you go under the door just like a little bug. *(She gives him her hands and he helps her up.)*

ALICE: *(Wiping it off her dress.)* Would you like some? *(He shakes his head.)* No, I didn't think so.

LEWIS: No, thank you . . . eat the cake, eat the cake . . . *(In march tempo.)* Eeeeat the cake, eat the cake, eeeeeat the cake. *(The group under the table begins to create the sound of a parade band playing "Stars and Stripes.")*

ALICE: Which way? Which way?

LEWIS/AGENT: I am going to make you the biggest thing in the biggest parade in the biggest city in the world . . . now, what is the biggest thing in the biggest parade in the biggest city . . .

ALICE: The balloon.

LEWIS/AGENT: The balloon? Naah. The balloon princess! *(He blows her up, using her finger as a valve.)*

On the table that now rises fifty feet of sheer glass, straight up.

Because just before you fell, I saw this magnificent chocolate layer cake with fudge frosting . . .

131

ALICE: Me? . . . Yeah, me. *(She inflates herself till all her body is extended.)* Not too big. Not too big. *(Lewis stops blowing her up and begins marching and twirling a baton in front of her.)* Who are you?

LEWIS: I'm the Drum Major.

ALICE: Oh yes, we need a drum major . . . down there . . . at my feet . . . I'm the biggest thing in this parade.

LEWIS: *(The music dies down.)* You want to be bigger than me?

ALICE: I'm the balloon princess.

LEWIS: You want to be bigger than ME.

ALICE: Yes . . . hello down there . . . you said. *(Lewis gets down on his back at her feet.)*

The balloon princess!

LEWIS: Hurray . . . *(The other actors cheer the princess with Lewis.)* . . . hurray for Alice . . . Aaaaalice.

ALICE: Yes.

LEWIS: This is your feet . . . get the little key.

ALICE: Oh, yes. *(Leans down and gets the key.)* . . . I have the little key.

LEWIS: Open the little door.

ALICE: Open the little door.

LEWIS: No, here . . . at your feet. *(Makes little door with his fingers.)*

ALICE: Yeah . . . okay. *(She gets down and opens the door. Lewis makes music in a tiny voice—"Stars and Stripes.")* Okay for you . . . I'm not playing with you anymore *(Lewis begins to create the rabbit by cupping his hand and speaking in a small rabbit's voice.)* . . . because you cheat.

. . . hello down there . . .

LEWIS/RABBIT: Oh my ears and whiskers . . . oh dear, I shall be late . . . oh, the Duchess . . . the Duchess will have my head . . . oh, my ears . . . my . . .

ALICE: I don't care about your ears. . . . I . . . oh, no . . . is that the . . . *(She kneels down and takes Lewis' hand and moves it away, revealing the rabbit.)* . . . oh . . . oh, excuse me sir. . . .

LEWIS/RABBIT: Oh, . . . oh . . . aaaaaaaaah. Giant. Thump. Thump. Thump. Thump. Creak, slam, bam, click, bar, bolt, lock.

ALICE: *(Throwing herself to the floor and pounding the ground with her fists.)* Nooooooo! *(Lewis imitates her movements, thereby setting up a mirror image throughout the following speech.)*

ALICE/LEWIS: *(Together.)* Oh, dear . . . oh, dear . . . how queer everything is today. I wonder if I could have been changed in the night? But if I'm not the same . . . the next question is . . . who in the world am I? I know I can't be Mabel . . . because I know so many things and she . . . oh, she knows such a very little. And besides, she's she and I'm, I. . . . I'll try and see if I know all the things I used to know. . . . *(At this point Lewis' voice gets higher and Alice's voice gets lower.)* . . . four times five is twenty/twelve, four times six is twenty-four/thirteen, four times seven is twenty-eight/fourteen, four times eight . . . oh, dear that can't be right . . . I must have been changed for Mabel. *(Alice freezes and Lewis takes her on his knee and makes her a ventriloquist's dummy.)*

LEWIS: Oooooh, I'll try. "How Doth the Little . . ."

ALICE/DUMMY: *(In a very deep and hoarse voice.)* How doth the little crocodile improve his shining tail, and pour the waters of the Nile on every golden scale. How cheerfully he seems to grin, how neatly spreads his claws, and welcomes little fishes in with gently smiling jaws. *(Lewis makes Alice/Dummy bow and then pulls on imaginary strings, making her into a marionette.)*

LEWIS/PUPPETEER: Oh, dear, I must be Mabel after all.

ALICE/PUPPET: *(In very high voice.)* No, I've made up my mind. If I'm Mabel I'll stay down here.

LEWIS/PUPPETEER: It'll be no use their poking their heads down and saying, "Come up, dear" . . .

ALICE/PUPPET: For I will only look up and say, "Tell me who I am then. And if I like being that person then I'll come up. . . ."

LEWIS/PUPPETEER: "And if not, I'll stay right down here 'till I'm somebody else."

ALICE: Oh, no. It's no use pretending to be two people now. I do wish they'd put their heads down . . . I'm very tired of being alone down here. *(Lewis claps his hands together, thereby cutting the strings, and Alice collapses to the ground.)* Noooooooo.

LEWIS: Don't cry. . . . You'll be very sorry if you cry. It isn't a very pretty sight, a great, huge girl like you crying, you know.

ALICE: No? *(She turns to face him and cries all the louder.)*

LEWIS: What do you want? *(She throws herself into his arms.)* Oh, you're lonely . . . you want a playmate . . . a playmate for the balloon princess. *(He begins to blow himself up.)*

ALICE: Not for her . . . she was too big for him. . . . *(He becomes totally inflated.)* . . . What's that?

. . . and welcome little fishes in with gently smiling jaws.

If I'm Mabel I'll stay down here.

LEWIS: Das is der Dirigible Prinz.

ALICE: I don't want the Dirigible Prince.

LEWIS: Jah. Guten tag, mein frau. . . .

ALICE: No. I don't want him. *(She hits him and punctures him. Lewis deflates and collapses onto the floor.)* I'm sorry . . . I don't want to be bigger than you. I don't want to be the balloon princess. . . . I was bad. Look I'll punish myself. *(She begins to box her own ears.)* See . . . sssssss, sssssssssss . . . sssss. *(She puts her hands over her ears and the deflating stops, but when she takes them away she deflates.)*

LEWIS: *(Lewis' arm slowly rises and waves in front of her face.)* Sssssssssssee.

ALICE: See what?

LEWIS: Sssssssssea serpent.

ALICE: No there can't be a sea serpent. There is no sea. Not in a hall.

LEWIS: Yes, salt sea. Sea of tears . . . your tears.

ALICE: Go away.

LEWIS: Swim.

ALICE: I can't. . . . I'll drown. *(Lewis/sea serpent comes closer.)*

LEWIS: Swim. *(She does and the group starts to make sea sounds as Larry and Jerry make music: "By the sea, by the sea . . .") (There is a blackout as Alice disappears under the table while making desperate swimming motions. The following scene is played in the dark. Sea sounds.)*

ALICE: Mouse . . . oh, mouse . . . do you know the way out of this sea? Oh, mouse. Oh, maybe he doesn't understand English? Maybe he's a French mouse. Où est ma chatte?

MOUSE: *(Screams.)*

ALICE: Oh, I beg your pardon. I quite forgot, you didn't like cats.

LEWIS: Not like cats. Would you like cats if you were me?

ALICE: Well, no, perhaps not, but please, don't be angry. I wish I could show you my cat, Dinah. She's a nice soft, gentle little thing. And she's a capital one for catching mice. . . . *(The Mouse screams.)* Oh, I'm sorry. We won't talk about her anymore if you don't like.

MOUSE: We? We, indeed. As if I would ever talk on such a subject. Our family

I don't want the Dirigible Prince.

See . . . sssssss, sssssssssss . . .

has always hated cats. They're nasty, low, mean, vulgar creatures. Don't you ever let me hear you mention them again.

ALICE: I won't, indeed. *(Pause. Sea sounds.)* Are you fond of dogs?

MOUSE: *(Screams.)* I'll take you to shore. . . .

ALICE: You will?

MOUSE: . . . and tell you my history, and then maybe you'll understand why it is that I hate cats and dogs. *(Lights come on dimly and a group of animals is discovered huddled together with Alice in the middle. There is a duck, crab, lory, dodo, and the mouse. They are all wet and uncomfortable.)* William the Conqueror, whose cause was favored by the Pope, was soon submitted to by the English, who wanted leaders, and who were much accustomed as of late to usurpation and conquest. Now, Edwin and Morcar, the Earls of Mercia and Northumbria . . . *(Lory shrieks.)* I beg your pardon . . . did you speak?

I beg your pardon . . . did you speak?

LORY: Not I.

MOUSE: Oh, I thought you did. I proceed. Edwin and Morcar, the Earls of Mercia and Northumbria, soon declared for him, and even Stigand, the patriotic Archbishop of Canterbury, found it advisable to go with . . .

DUCK: Found what?

MOUSE: Found IT. Of course, you know what it means.

DUCK: It's frogs and worms when I find a thing.

ALICE: I think the Duck would like to know what it is the Archbishop found.

MOUSE: He found it ADVISABLE . . . to go with Edgar Atheling and offer him the crown . . . now, William's conduct at first was moderate. But the insolence of his Normans. . . . *(The animals become restless and the Crab and Lory shriek.)* . . . ooooooh . . . how are you getting on, my dear?

ALICE: I'm as wet as ever. *(The others agree.)*

MOUSE: But it's the driest thing I know.

ALICE: Well, I'm afraid it doesn't seem to dry me a bit.

DODO: Uhh, then I suggest that we adjourn the meeting for the adoption of more energetic remedies. *(The group all huddle around the Dodo.)*

LORY: Speak English. I don't understand a word of what you are saying.

DODO: I was about to say, that the best thing to get us dry would be a caw . . . caw . . . awww, . . . caucus race?

ALICE: What's a caucus race?

DODO: The best way to show you is to do it.

LORY: Dooooo it. Doooo it. . . . *(They run the race in place, advancing very slightly as one takes the lead and then another. The Dodo, who is last, starts to run backwards until he is behind the paper curtain.)*

DODO: *(As he reappears.)* The race is over.

ALL: *(Crowding around the Dodo.)* Who won? Who won?

DODO: I . . . I . . . I . . . I . . .

CRAB: Who?

DODO: I . . . think that everybody won . . . and all must have prizes. *(To Alice.)* She must give prizes.

ALICE: But I don't have any. . . .

ALL: *(Closing in on Alice.)* Prizes. Prizes.

ALICE: I think I have come comfits. *(She reaches into her pocket and gives them.)*

CRAB: Comfits. *(They eat them. Each tries to enjoy them but either they choke or find them distasteful.)*

MOUSE: She must have prizes also.

DODO: What else have you got? *(They all close in on her again.)*

ALICE: I have a thimble.

DODO: Give it there. *(She hands it to the crab.)* We would love to present you with this elegant dimblo.

CRAB: Eat it.

ALICE: But you don't eat thimbles.

CRAB: We ate the comfits.

ALICE: *(Turning to the mouse for help.)* You promised to tell us your history and why it is that you hate cats and dogs. *(All crowd around mouse, screaming,"Story, story.")*

MOUSE: Mine is a long and a sad tale.

ALICE: Oh, long and sad. We'd better sit down.

LORY: Sit.

Doooooo it. Dooooo it.

ALICE: *(To Lory.)* Yes, sit.

LORY: Sit.

ALICE: Sit.

MOUSE: SIT. *(All sit and come to order after a few shouts of "Story, story.")* Fury said to a mouse that he met in the house, "Let us both go to law: I will prosecute you—" *(He points to Duck.)*

DUCK: Wheeeee.

MOUSE: "Come, I'll take no denial; we must have a trial: for really this morning I've nothing to do'…"

DUCK: *(To Alice.)* Why don't you take off your clothes?

MOUSE: *(Continues after regaining order.)* … "Said the mouse to the cur, 'Such a trial, dear sir, with no jury or judge, would be wasting our breath!' 'I'll be judge, I'll be jury,' said cunning old fury: 'I'll try the whole cause and condemn you to death.'" *(During this portion of the story, the Dodo and Alice have become involved in a conversation.)* … You. *(To Alice.)* You're not attending. What can you be thinking of?

LORY: *(To Alice.)* Death … death … death.

ALICE: I was attending … you had gotten to the fifth bend, I think.

MOUSE: I had not.

ALICE: Oh, a knot. Let me help you undo it.

MOUSE: I'll do nothing of the sort. Your conduct offends me very much. *(Exits.)*

ALICE: It was a joke. You're easily offended, you know.

LORY: What a pity it wouldn't stay. That should be a lesson to you, my dear, never to lose your temper.

CRAB: Story. Story. What about the story?

ALICE: Me? It was the mouse who lost his temper.

LORY: No, you are enough to try the patience of an oyster.

ALICE: The Dodo asked me a question and I simply answered him.

DUCK: *(Pulling at Alice's dress.)* Why don't you take off your clothes?

LORY: I am older than you and must know better.

ALICE: Oh yes? How old are you?

Fury said to a mouse …

LORY: How old are you?

ALICE: How old are *you?*

LORY: How old are *you?*

ALICE: I asked you first . . . oh, I wish I had Dinah here. . . .

CRAB: *(Who has been encouraging the Lory to fight all along.)* Who's Dinah?

LORY: Who's Dinah, if I might venture to ask the question.

ALICE: You might venture . . . Dinah's my cat.

LORY: Dinah's my . . . CAT! *(Screams.)*

ALICE: Oh, she loves little birds. Why you should see her after the little birds . . . *(Lory exits shrieking.)*

CRAB: CAT! *(As he exits by way of the audience.)* Excuse me! *(The Duck has also left and the Dodo and Alice are left together.)*

ALICE: *(To Lory as she exits.)* Bye. *(To Dodo.)* I took care of her.

DODO: Cad?

ALICE: No, cat, You know. . . . *(Dodo begins to leave.)* . . . No, no, not you. . . . I'm sure Dinah's the best cat in the whole world.

DODO: *(From off stage.)* Do-do.

ALICE: *(Left completely alone.)* Yeah. Dodo. Oh, Dinah, my dear. I wonder if I shall ever see you again? *(Actors begin to reappear one by one and surround Alice.)*

GERRY: Ooooh, my dear paws.

LARRY: She'll have me executed.

TOM: The Duchess, the Duchess.

SASKIA: She'll have me executed. . . .

JERRY: She'll have me executed.

LARRY: *(Extending his arms over Alice to form a roof.)* Eeeeeeeeeeeeeaaaaaaaah. A neat little house.

ALL: *(Except Alice — each actor makes part of the house until Alice is entrapped.)* A neat little house, a neat little house . . . *(The house slowly pushes Alice to the ground.)* . . . a neat little house.

ALICE: *(As she collapses to the ground.)* It was much pleasanter at home. When

A neat little house.

one wasn't always growing larger and smaller . . . you know, I almost wish I hadn't gone down that hole . . . and yet, it is rather curious this sort of life.

GERRY: Never get out again.

TOM: Came an angry voice.

SASKIA: Keep her neck from being broken.

TOM: Came an angry voice.

LARRY: Trembled till she shook the house.

TOM: Came an angry voice.

ALICE: I think I can kick a little.

TOM: Came an ANGRY voice.

GERRY: Let's burn the house down.

ALL: *(Except Alice.)* Down. down. . . .

ALICE: Noooo. *(She kicks her way free and runs off.)* I'll put a stop to this. *(The actors who are left, think a moment, and then the idea of the mushroom hits — four actors form the mushroom. Larry climbs up on their backs and becomes the caterpillar, using Gerry's arm as his hookah which he puffs upon during the entire scene. As the mushroom is formed, Alice runs out behind the audience and re-enters on the other side of the playing area.)*

ALICE'S VOICE: *(As she runs around.)* First I've got to get back to my right size and then I can get into that lovely garden. Yes, that's the best plan . . . very simple and easy to arrange . . . if I could just think. Now, first my right size. But how is that to be managed? Oh, I know, I have to eat or drink something. But then the next question is what?

CATERPILLAR: *(Seeing Alice as she re-enters.)* Who are you?

ALICE: Well, I hardly know. I mean, just at present. You see, I know who I was when I got up this morning, but I've been changed several times since then.

CATERPILLAR: What do you mean by that? Explain yourself.

ALICE: I can't explain myself. I'm not myself, you see?

CATERPILLAR: I don't see.

ALICE: I'm afraid I can't put it anymore clearly than that. You see, I don't understand it myself to begin with. But it's being so many different sizes in a day . . . that's what's very confusing.

CATERPILLAR: No it isn't.

Let's burn the house down.

Noooo. I'll put a stop to this.

ALICE: Well, maybe you haven't found it so yet. But you just wait—you're going to have to change into a chrysalis . . . oh, you will someday, you know, and after that into a butterfly. You'll find that a little queer . . . won't you? *(Caterpillar uses his arms as wings and attempts to fly. Music: Jerry: "Un bel Di.")*

CATERPILLAR: *(Music ends.)* Wow . . . *(Pause.)* . . . not a bit.

ALICE: You are different. That would be very queer to me.

CATERPILLAR: You . . . who are you? *(Mushroom sniggers.)*

ALICE: I think you better tell me who you are first.

CATERPILLAR: Why? *(Alice begins to leave.)* Come back. I've got something important to say: Keep your temper.

ALICE: That's IT?

CATERPILLAR: Ahhh, no. You think you've changed?

ALICE: Yes, I've changed. I can't remember things the way I used to. I can't even keep the same size for more than ten minutes together.

CATERPILLAR: Can't remember . . . can't remember what things?

ALICE: Well, I tried to say "How Doth the Little Busy Bee." but it all came out different.

CATERPILLAR: Why don't you repeat, "You are old, Father William"?

ALICE: "You are old, Father William, the young man said, and your hair has become very white. Yet you incessantly stand on your head, at your age do you think that is right? In my youth, Father William replied to his son, I feared it might injure my brain. But now that I'm perfectly sure I have none, why I do it again and again." *(They both laugh.)*

CATERPILLAR: That wasn't said right.

ALICE: Not quite right. A few of the words got altered, that's all.

CATERPILLAR: Nooooooooo. That was wrong from the beginning to the end of it. *(He sticks out his tongue and Alice slaps him. He motions for her to come closer, Alice does so, resigned for her punishment, holding out her hand. The Caterpillar takes it and uses it to slap himself.)* Woooooow! What size did you want to be?

ALICE: Oh, I'm not particular as to the size . . . it's just that one doesn't like changing so often, you know?

CATERPILLAR: I don't know . . . are you happy?

ALICE: No. I'd like to be a little larger, if you don't mind, sir. Three inches is a wretched height to be.

. . . and after that into a butterfly . . .

You . . . who are you?

That was wrong from the beginning to the end of it.

CATERPILLAR: You'll get used to it in time. One side makes you grow taller and the other side makes you grow smaller. *(As Alice looks from side to side, the Caterpillar slips into the center of the mushroom and only his voice is heard coming up from inside.)* The Mushroom!

MUSHROOM: *(Singing Holy Om.)* Aaaaaaaaaaaaaoooooooooooohhhhhhhhhhhhmmmmmmmmmm aaaaaaaaaoooooohhhhhhhhm *(Alice climbs up on top of the mushroom.)*

ALICE: But which side is which? *(The hand of one actor who is part of the mushroom reaches up towards her and she takes a bite of it. Then she reaches down and picks up the hookah and takes a puff. The mushroom grows louder and begins to sway. As she reclines on the mushroom.)* Wow!

JERRY: *(In an oriental voice.)* Suddenly she felt a sharp blow beneath her chin. She was shrinking so rapidly her chin had struck her foot . . . so she set about to eat some of the other side.

ALICE: *(She does so.)* My head's free.

JERRY: But when she looked down all she could see was an immense length of neck, rising like a stalk which would bend about easily in any direction, just like a . . .

ALICE: Like a serpent.

JERRY: SSSSSSSerpent . . . sssssshhhhhhhhhh. . . .

ALL: SSSsssssssssssshhhhhhhhh *(Alice is gently lowered to the ground where she curls up to sleep in a fetal position. The rest quietly set about creating the Duchess's house by placing the table over three of the actors who are to play the Duchess, the Cheshire Cat and the Cook. Chairs stacked up serve as the chimney at the side of the table. One actor, who plays the Frog footman, stations himself in front of the house, and the other actor goes behind the Duchess and creates the cries of her baby, which is a doll that the Duchess holds. Throughout the scene the doll is flung from person to person like a game of "hot potato," and there is constant cacophony due to the baby's cries and the Cook's banging on a pipe which represents a soup caldron. He uses a can of talcum powder as a pepper shaker. Alice wakes upon the first bang and taps the Frog footman on the shoulder to get his attention. He croaks and jumps up. Alice taps him again and he jumps again. Finally, on the third tap, he speaks.)*

FROG: There's no use in knocking, you know, because I'm on the same side of the door as you are.

ALICE: Then, please, how am I to get into the house?

FROG: Now, if we had the door between us, there might be some good in your knocking, you know.

What size did you want to be?

. . . are you happy?

My head's free.

ALICE: How am I to get in?

FROG: Are you to get in at all? That's the first question, you know.

ALICE: But what am I to do?

FROG: Anything you like.

ALICE: Anything I like?

FROG: Anything you like. *(Alice enters the house.)*

ALICE: Aaaaaachoo. There's certainly too much pepper in your soup. Would you please tell me why your cat grins like that?

DUCHESS: It's a Cheshire cat and that's why. *(Alice sneezes. To baby.)* Pig.

ALICE: I never knew that Cheshire cats always grinned. I never knew that cats could grin at all.

DUCHESS: All of them can and most of them do. Aaaaaachoo.

ALICE: Aaaaaaachoo. I never knew any who did.

DUCHESS: You don't know much and that's a fact.

ALICE: *(To Frog who has just hit her with the baby.)* Hey, watch what you're doing. You almost hurt the baby.

DUCHESS: If everybody minded their own business, the world would go round a great deal faster than it does.

ALICE: That wouldn't be any advantage, you know. Just think what would happen with the day and the night. You see, the world takes twenty-four hours to go around on its axis. . . .

DUCHESS: Speaking of axis, chop off her head! *(At this point the baby, which has been tossed out of the house by the cook, is jumped on by the frog and punted back to the Duchess. The actor who has been creating the baby's cries rises from behind the table and begins to wildly conduct as the cook beats out the rhythm and the Duchess sings in tune of "Anvil Chorus.")* I speak severely to my boy and beat him when he sneezes, for he can thoroughly enjoy the pepper when he pleases.

ALL: For he can thoroughly enjoy the pepper when he pleases. Wow, wow, wow. Wow, wow wow. Wow, wwwa-wow, wwwwa-wow.

DUCHESS: Here, you may nurse it a bit if you like.

ALICE: No. . . . thank you.

DUCHESS: I must go and get ready to play croquet with the queen.

Anything you like.

. . . please tell me why your cat grins like that?

ALICE: (Taking the baby.) Wow!

DUCHESS: (Exiting.) Wow!

FROG: (As Duchess passes.) Wow!

ALICE: (Escaping from house—to Frog.) I had to take the baby.

FROG: Wow!

ALICE: No, it would have been murder. if I had left it in there another minute.

FROG: Wow!

ALICE: What am I going to do with a baby when I get it home?

FROG: Anything you like.

ALICE: Anything I like?

FROG: Anything. . . .

ALICE: Thanks. Come on, baby. (As she starts to exit through audience, she snorts.) You mustn't grunt, baby. That's no way to express yourself. (Snorts again.) Now, if you're going to turn into a little pig, I'll have nothing more to do with you. (Snorts again.) I warned you, baby. (Gives the doll to one of the audience members.) It was an ugly child. It makes a rather handsome pig, I think. (The Cheshire cat appears up on the table during the time Alice has been busy with the doll. The stack of chairs has also been placed around the table by the other actors and the table has been set for the "Mad Tea Party." When Alice turns she finds a frozen tableau of the Mad Hatter, March Hare and Dormouse seated at the table. The only mobile person is the cat, who moves and speaks in a mechanical way.)

CAT: Mroowrrrrr.

ALICE: Oh, Cheshire Cat. Can you (As Alice approaches him, his paw goes up as if to strike if she gets too close.) . . . please tell me which way I ought to go from here?

CAT: Well, that depends a great deal on where you want to get to.

ALICE: I guess I don't much care where.

CAT: Then it doesn't matter very much which way you go.

ALICE: As long as I get somewhere.

CAT: Oh, you're bound to do that, if only you walk far enough. (Laughs hysterically.)

ALICE: Could you tell me the kind of people that live around here?

I speak severely to my boy
and beat him when he sneezes . . .

CAT: Well, in that direction *(Points at the Hatter.)* lives a Mad Hatter, and in that direction *(Points at the Hare.)* lives a March Hare. Visit either one you like; they're both of them mad.

ALICE: I don't want to go among mad people.

CAT: Oh, you can't help that. We're all of us mad here. I'm mad and you're mad.

ALICE: How do you know I'm mad?

CAT: You must be mad or you wouldn't have come here. *(Laughs so hard, he falls over. Alice helps him up and tries to sit next to him but he raises his paw again.)* Bye the bye, what ever became of the baby? I'd nearly forgotten to ask.

ALICE: It turned into a pig. *(Cat laughs and motions her to sit by him.)* You're crazy. *(She sits up on the table next to him.)*

CAT: I told you so. Did you say pig or fig? *(Laughing uncontrollably.)*

ALICE: I said PIG. *(Laughs.)*

CAT: *(Stopping laughing abruptly.)* I don't think that's one bit funny. *(At this point the tableau around the table comes to life and the Mad Hatter slams his fist down on the table, shouting:)*

HATTER: NO ROOM. NO ROOM. *(Both Alice and the Cat jump off the table and run.)*

HARE: No, no, no, no . . . no room there; there's room here. *(Taps place by him.)*

HATTER: No room . . . no . . .

ALICE: There's plenty of room . . . *(Moving chair over near Hare.)*

HARE: Would you like some wine! *(Takes imaginary bottle and pours.)* Glug . . . glug.

ALICE: I don't see any wine.

HARE: There isn't any.

ALICE: Then it wasn't very civil of you to offer it.

HARE: It wasn't very civil of you to sit down without being asked, now was it?

ALICE: *(To Hatter.)* I'm sorry . . . I didn't know it was your table. It's much larger than for three, you know.

HATTER: You know, your hair needs cutting. *(Hare throws torn paper up in the air. Dormouse throws a spitball at him. Hare hits Dormouse over the head with loaf of french bread. Hatter quiets them.)*

We're all of us mad here.

NO ROOM. NO ROOM.

ALICE: You should learn not to make personal remarks; they're very rude.

HATTER: Ahh, then why is a raven like a writing desk?

ALICE: Riddles. I like riddles.

HARE: Because the notes. . . .

HATTER: Ahhh!

ALICE: No, that's all right. I think I can guess the answer to that one.

HARE: You mean, you think you can find out the answer to that riddle?

ALICE: Yes. Exactly.

HARE: Then you should say what you mean. *(Juggles bread.)*

ALICE: Oh, I do. Well, at least I mean what I say. It's the same thing, you know.

HARE: Oh, no, no. . . .

HATTER: No, it's not the same thing, not the same thing at all. You might just as well say . . .

DORMOUSE: You might just as well say . . . *(Hare shoves bread in his mouth.)*

HATTER: . . . Not the same thing a bit . . . you might just as well say that I see what I eat, is the same thing as I eat what I see.

HARE: You might just . . .

DORMOUSE: You might just as well say . . . *(Hare shoves bread in his mouth.)*

HARE: You might just as well say that I like what I get is the same thing as I get what I like. *(Hatter snaps his fingers and motions to the Dormouse. Hare whispers.)* Yes, now.

DORMOUSE: You might just as well say . . . *(Dormouse forgets and Hare bangs on Dormouse's army helmet with a spoon.)* . . . you might just as well say that I sleep when I breathe is the same thing as I breathe when I sleep.

HATTER: Yes. Of course, it is the same for you. *(All laugh. The Dormouse becomes excited and screams, lunging at Alice with a spoon. She falls off her seat while the Dormouse is controlled by the two others.)* You wouldn't happen to know to-day's date?

ALICE: The date? . . . uhhh . . . it's . . .

HARE: *(Whispers.)* The thirty-second.

ALICE: The thirty-second . . . no . . . it's the *(Present date.)* I think.

It wasn't very civil of you to sit down without being asked, now was it?

You know, your hair needs cutting.

HATTER: The *(Present date.)*? I'm two days wrong. I told you butter wouldn't suit the works.

HARE: It was the best butter, you know.

ALICE: *(To Hare.)* You put butter in his watch? *(Hare nods.)*

HATTER: *(To Hare.)* Yes, but you got crumbs in it, I told you not to use the bread-knife.

HARE: But it was the best butter.

ALICE: *(Crossing to Hatter to better see his watch.)* He put butter in your watch? You let him put butter in your watch? *(Laughs.)*

HATTER: Yes . . . but he got crumbs . . . I told him not to use the bread-knife . . . . . . why are you . . . *(Alice leans on his shoulder to help her stand because she is laughing so hard; the Hatter becomes very upset and begins to squeeze the butter. When Alice realizes this she tries to control her laughter.)*

ALICE: It's a funny watch.

HATTER: Funny?

ALICE: It tells you what day of the month it is, but it doesn't tell you what o'clock it is.

HATTER: Why should it? Does your watch tell you what year it is?

ALICE: No. But it stays the same year a very long time, you know.

HATTER: Just the case with mine.

ALICE: I beg your pardon?

Of course, it is the same for you.

HATTER: *(Realizing that he has squeezed the butter to the point of its oozing out of the package, he loses control and smashes the butter into the Dormouse's face. To Alice who has quickly taken her seat again.)* He was asleep again . . . musn't sleep at table. . . . *(Trying to regain composure.)* Did you guess the answer to that riddle yet?

HARE: Because Poe wrote on both. . . . *(Hatter screams.)*

ALICE: No, I give up. . . . I give up . . . what's the answer?

HATTER: I haven't the faintest idea.

HARE: Nor I. . . .

ALICE: I think you two would have better things to do with your time than wasting it by asking me riddles that don't have an answer.

He was asleep again . . . mustn't sleep at table . . .

HATTER: If you knew time as well as I, you wouldn't refer to IT, it's HIM.

ALICE: I don't understand you.

HATTER: No. I daresay you don't . . . *(The Hare gets Alice's attention and motions to her that the Hatter is crazy. The Hatter sees this and Hare turns signal into another motion.)* I daresay you've never even spoken to Time.

ALICE: Spoken? *(Hare motions "no" to Alice.)* No, no I haven't, but I know that I have to beat time when I learn music. *(She bangs in time on the table. Music: Alice, March Hare and Dormouse: "El Rancho Rio Grande." Alice and Hare do a flamenco.)*

I daresay you've never even spoken to Time.

HATTER: Ah that accounts for it. . . . *(When he realizes that things are getting out of his control, he screams and all sit.)* . . . He won't stand beating. If you could just stay on his good side, you know he'd do almost anything you liked . . . uh, with the clock, I . . . suppose it were nine o'clock in the morning . . . time for you to start your lessons . . . well, all you'd have to do is just whisper a little word to Time . . . and around would go the hands of the clock in a twinkling . . . to . . . half-past one, maybe . . . time for dinner. . . .

HARE: *(Who has been playing footsie with Alice under the table.)* I wish it were.

ALICE: You wouldn't be hungry for it then.

HATTER: Perhaps not . . . but you could keep it there just as long as you liked.

ALICE: Is that how you manage?

HARE: Pssssssst . . . huh-huh.

HATTER: No, that is not how I manage . . . we quarrelled . . . Time and I . . . some time ago . . . *(Seeing that the Hare is making time with Alice.)* . . . just last March it was . . . just before HE *(Pointing to Hare.)* went mad.

ALICE: HIM? *(Pointing.)*

HATTER: Him. *(Hare motions that Hatter's the crazy one.)*

ALICE: Oh, yes . . . yes.

HATTER: It's true. . . . I was there; I saw it . . . it was at the concert given by the Queen of Hearts. . . . I had to sing, "Twinkle, Twinkle, Little Bat." You know that song? *(Dormouse begins to sing to the tune of "The Missouri Waltz.")*

ALICE: Yes, I know something like it.

HATTER: Well, I hadn't even finished. . . . *(To Dormouse, who is singing.)* Yes, that's it. *(He joins the Dormouse in singing while Hare and Alice dance. All sing:)*

ALL: Twinkle, twinkle, twinkle, twinkle, twinkle little bat.... *(The Dormouse gets up on the table, playing an imaginary violin, while Alice and Hare waltz. The Hatter tries to cut in but the Hare whisks Alice past. The Dormouse laughs and the Hatter turns the table over, throwing the Dormouse to the floor.)*

HATTER: Get off ... GET ... GET OFF. *(Dormouse runs under the table.)* Come out of there ... come out ... out ... out ... out. *(In his rage, the Hatter climbs up onto the table and beats on it with his fists and feet.)*

HARE: *(Applauding.)* VERY nice....

HATTER: *(Regaining his composure, climbs off the table and back into his seat. Others sit.)* Noo ... at any event, I hadn't even finished singing the first verse, when the Queen suddenly bawled out, "Him.... He's murdering the Time. Off with his head." Ever since then, he won't do a thing that I ask, Time, it's always six o'clock now.... Time for tea ... time for tea....

HARE: *(Who has been pushed off his chair by the Dormouse, who has been trying to get Alice's attention.)* All right. I think we ought to change the subject ... I'm ... *(To Hatter.)* ... getting tired of this one. I vote the young lady tells us a story.

HATTER: Oh, yes.

ALICE: I'm afraid I don't know any stories. I'm sorry.

HARE: Then the Dormouse shall. Wake up, Dormouse. Tell us a story.

DORMOUSE: I wasn't asleep.

HATTER: No, no, no.

ALICE: It's all right; see, he's going to tell us a story.

DORMOUSE: *(Who has gotten up on the table.)* Once upon a time.

ALICE: See, it's all right. Go on.

HATTER: Nooooo.

HARE: GO ON.

DORMOUSE: Once upon a time, there were three little sisters ... and their names were ... Elsie *(Points to Hatter.)* ... Lacey *(To Hare.)*, and Tillie ...

HARE: TILLIE. *(Also on table top.)*

HATTER: TILLIE.

DORMOUSE: ... and they lived at the bottom of a well.

Twinkle, twinkle, twinkle ...

Come out of there ... come out ...

ALICE: What did they live on? *(Admiring Hare, who is prancing around.)*

DORMOUSE: They lived on . . . *(Spits chewed-up bread at Hare.)* . . . treacle.

ALICE: They couldn't have lived on treacle; they would have been ill.

DORMOUSE: *(Jumping off table and throwing Alice to the ground.)* If you want to finish the story, finish the story.

ALICE: No, no. I won't interrupt anymore; I promise.

HARE: Have some more tea. *(Jumping off table and spitting at Dormouse.)*

HATTER: Yes, do. Have some more tea. . . .

ALICE: I've had nothing at this stupid party; how can I have more?

HATTER: No, you mean how can you have less? It's very easy to take more than nothing.

ALICE: Nobody asked your opinion.

HATTER: Who's making the personal remarks now? *(The Hare and the Dormouse stage a gunfight. Music: "High Noon." The Hare distracts the Dormouse by pointing, and then shoots him. The Hare triumphantly poses on table. Alice goes and sits on the table next to him and the Dormouse turns the table over.)*

DORMOUSE: And they were learning to draw.

ALICE: What did they draw?

DORMOUSE: They drew everything that begins with an "M."

ALICE: Why with an "M"?

DORMOUSE: Why not?. . . . Everything . . . like moonlight . . . and memory . . . and . . .

ALICE: Mushrooms . . . that begins with an "M."

DORMOUSE: And muchness . . . you know you say things are "much of a muchness" . . . have you ever seen such a thing as a drawing of a muchness?

ALICE: A drawing? . . . No, no I haven't. *(Dormouse pulls a piece of chalk from his pocket and joins the Hare who is writing on the overturned table. The table has now become the wall of the Queen of Heart's Garden. To Hatter.)* He's drawing a muchness.

HATTER: I know. *(The Dormouse starts to draw the body of a naked woman but Alice grabs the chalk.)*

ALICE: No, . . . it's . . . it's a teapot. *(She turns Dormouse's drawing into a teapot.)*

Once upon a time.

. . . there were three little sisters . . .

HATTER: A teapot? It's a teapot . . . a Dormouse-teapot . . . and you're going in it . . . in, in, in . . . *(He drags the Dormouse over behind the table, shoving him into the "teapot." Then, he runs around table and joins Hare and Alice, who are writing on table top. Music: "Stars and Stripes," while writing graffiti. Graffiti: "T. Dum & T. Dee" in a heart, "Alice eats Mushrooms," "Lewis likes Liddell Girls," etc.) (There is a whistle from off stage and the Hatter and Hare scream, "The Queen of Hearts" and leap over the table and hide.)*

ALICE: *(Reading graffiti.)* "Kings are white, Queens are red, when the Queen sees you, 'Off with your head'" *(Hatter, Dormouse, and Hare—Jerry, Larry, and Gerry, have become Queen's Gardeners. Music. They sing: "Hail to the Chief." The three men sink behind table again as the King and Queen enter.)*

RED QUEEN: *(To Alice.)* Who's this?

ALICE: My name is Alice. So please your majesty. *(Alice curtseys deeply and King taps her on the rear.)* . . . sties.

RED QUEEN: And what is this? *(Hitting table with her mallet.)*

ALICE: How should I know? It's no business of mine. *(The Queen motions with hand across throat.)*

KING: That means off with your head.

ALICE: Well, do something.

KING: Consider, my dear, she's only a child.

GARDENERS: *(Popping up from behind the table.)* Consider, my dear, she's only a child. *(The Queen goes berserk hitting all the men and some of the audience members shouting, "Off with their heads." The men try to calm her with, "Consider, my dear, she's only a child," but when that doesn't work, the King smacks her on the rear with his mallet.)*

KING: . . . Uh . . . let's play croquet.

RED QUEEN: *(To Alice.)* Can you play croquet?

GARDENER 1: No.

GARDENER 2: No.

GARDENER 3: No.

ALICE: . . . Uh . . . yeah, I can play croquet.

GARDENERS: *(Together.)* Ohhhh, no . . . ohh, ohhh. *(The King hands Alice his mallet and tries to escape.)*

RED QUEEN: Come on, then. *(Gardeners remove the "wall" turning it into the*

Stake.

"gate" of the Garden. All enter the Garden and the Croquet Field. Over the gramophone comes music from "Jules et Jim.") Stake. *(Pounding the King into the ground.)* Wicket. Wicket. Wicket. Ball. Ball. Ball. *(She bops the men with her mallet to make them take their places as the wickets and balls.)*

ALICE: *(Bops Jerry.)* Ball.

JERRY/ALICE'S BALL: Now, quit that.

ALICE: I'm sorry. Did I hurt you? I didn't mean . . . *(He curls up in his place.)*

RED QUEEN: Your turn.

GERRY/QUEEN'S BALL: Guests first.

ALICE: Oh, no. After you, your Majesty.

JERRY/ALICE'S BALL: Queens first. Royalty precedes . . .

RED QUEEN: No, no, no. After you . . . after you.

ALICE: Well, thank you. If you insist . . . *(The Queen shoots first.)* Good shot, your Majesty.

GERRY/QUEEN'S BALL: *(Missing wicket on purpose, turns to Queen and sticks out his tongue.)* Nyaaaaah.

RED QUEEN: Off with his head.

ALICE: My turn. *(She makes her shot; her ball goes through wicket.)* We go again.

RED QUEEN: No, it's my turn now.

ALICE: But my ball went through the wicket . . . you go again if it goes . . .

RED QUEEN: You don't know the rules of the game. *(Starts to shoot.)*

ALICE: You don't know. *(They shoot together, both screaming "BALL." The two balls collide with the wicket.)*

JERRY: Hey, we had the right-of-way. It was our turn.

GERRY. I'm the Queen's ball . . . *(He gets bopped by both the Queen and Alice.)*

RED QUEEN: Off with their heads . . . ball. *(She sends Gerry through the wicket.)*

ALICE: *(Grabbing the wicket [Larry] and pulling him towards her.)* No. It's my turn.

RED QUEEN: *(Grabbing him back.)* It's my turn. *(A tug of war with the wicket ensues as the women fight over whose turn it is. Queen bops Alice on the head.)* Off with your head.

Nyaaaaan.

My turn.

ALICE: Off with *YOUR* head. *(They stalk each other.)*

RED QUEEN: *(Hitting Alice.)* Off with your head.

ALICE: *(Hitting the Queen.)* Nonsense. *(The Queen and Alice freeze. The men create a forest by placing an umbrella with slits in it in front of the only light source, which gives the effect of light filtering through the trees. Each one takes an umbrella and uses it to become a tree; forest sounds. Larry takes an old sink leg and uses it to make loud snoring noises. Freeze ends and the Red Queen disappears.)* I wonder if there are any lions or tigers around here?

FOREST: No, that's just the Red King snoring. He's dreaming now. What do you suppose he's dreaming about?

ALICE: No one can guess that.

FOREST: Why about you. If that there King were to leave off dreaming, where do you suppose you'd be?

ALICE: Right where I am now, of course.

FOREST: Not you. You'd be nowhere. You're nothing but a sort of thing in his dream. If that there king were to wake, you'd go out bang just like a candle.

ALICE: No, I wouldn't.

FOREST: You know very well you're not real.

ALICE: No, I'm real.

FOREST: Shouting won't make you a bit more real, y'know. I hope you don't suppose those are real shouts. Real shouts: *(They shout. Alice screams and collapses under one of the trees; pause; forest sounds from under the umbrellas. The White Queen rushes on and catches her shawl on a branch of the tree under which Alice is hiding. Alice sees the shawl and cautiously comes out.)*

ALICE: Am I addressing the White Queen?

WHITE QUEEN: Well yes, if you call that addressing. It isn't my notion of the thing at all.

ALICE: Well, if your Majesty will just tell me the right way to begin, I'll be very glad to try to do it, as best as I can.

WHITE QUEEN: But I don't want it done at all. I've been a-dressing myself for the last two hours.

ALICE: May I help you on with your shawl?

WHITE QUEEN: I don't know what's the matter with it. I think it's out of temper. I've pinned it here and I've pinned it there, but there is no pleasing it.

I'm the Queen's ball . . .

It's my turn.

Off with YOUR head.

ALICE: May I? If you pin it in the middle. See. *(Notices the state the Queen's hair is in and fixes it.)* There, you look better now. But really, you ought to get yourself a lady's maid.

WHITE QUEEN: *(As an English Lady.)* I think I'll take you with pleasure. Tuppence a week and jam every other day.

ALICE: I don't want you to hire me. I don't like jam.

WHITE QUEEN: Oh, it's very good jam.

ALICE: I don't want any today, at any rate.

WHITE QUEEN: You couldn't have it if you did want it. You see, the rule is . . . *(She sings.)* jam tomorrow and jam yesterday, but never, never jam today.

ALICE: I don't understand. It's all very confusing.

WHITE QUEEN: Oh, that's the effect of living backwards. *(She spins around.)* It makes one a little giddy at first.

Am I addressing the White Queen?

ALICE: Living backwards?

WHITE QUEEN: Yes. *(As Marlene Dietrich.)* But there is a great advantage . . . and that is that your memory works both ways.

ALICE: I'm sure mine only works one way. . . . I can't remember things before they happen.

WHITE QUEEN: That's a very poor sort of memory that only works backwards. *(She wraps Alice's head with her shawl.)*

ALICE: Do you think you would tell me the kinds of things that you remember best?

WHITE QUEEN: Oh, . . . things that happened a week after next. For instance, there's the King's messenger. *(Holds up her finger and concentrates on it.)* He is in prison now being punished and the trial won't even begin till next Wednesday. And of course, the crime comes last of all.

ALICE: Suppose he doesn't commit the crime?

WHITE QUEEN: That would be all the better, wouldn't it?

ALICE: It wouldn't be all the better his being punished for it.

WHITE QUEEN: You are wrong there. Were you ever punished?

ALICE: Oh yes! but only for faults.

WHITE QUEEN: And you were all the better for it, I know.

I've been a-dressing myself for the last two hours.

ALICE: Yes . . . no, I had DONE the things I was punished for. It makes all the difference, you see?

WHITE QUEEN: Yes, but if you hadn't done them, that would have been better, and better and. . . . *(She grabs her finger and starts to scream.)*

ALICE: What's the matter?

WHITE QUEEN: My finger's bleeding.

ALICE: What happened? Did you prick it?

WHITE QUEEN: No, I haven't pricked it yet. But I soon shall.

ALICE: When do you intend to do it?

WHITE QUEEN. When I fasten my shawl again . . . *(Alice realizes she has the shawl, and she holds it out for the Queen, who approaches it cautiously.)*

ALICE: . . . Easy . . . be careful and you won't . . . no . . . *(Queen grabs shawl.)* you're holding it crooked. . . .

. . . no . . . you're holding it crooked . . .

WHITE QUEEN: *(Jabs herself, Alice helps her free her finger from the shawl.)* There. That accounts for the bleeding, you see. Now you understand the way things happen in here. *(Taps her head.)*

ALICE: Well, I'm glad it's over.

WHITE QUEEN: You must be very happy living in this wood and being glad whenever you like.

ALICE: Oh, no . . . no. It's very lonely.

WHITE QUEEN: Oh, no, don't go on like that . . . consider what a great girl you are, consider what a long way you have come today . . . consider what o'clock it is . . . consider anything. Let's consider my age to begin with. . . . I am . . . one hundred . . . and . . . one . . . five months and a day.

ALICE: I can't believe that.

WHITE QUEEN: Can't you? . . . Try again. Take a deep breath and shut your eyes.

ALICE: It's no use. You can't believe in impossible things.

WHITE QUEEN: I dare say you haven't had much practice. I used to do it for half an hour a day, . . . why, sometimes I have believed in as many as six impossible things before breakfast. *(During this speech the Queen has covered her face with her shawl and lowered her voice and stalked around like a monster. The forest sounds become more intense. When the Queen lifts the shawl and shows her face, Alice runs into her arms. The Queen wraps herself and Alice up in the shawl and they twirl around. The forest disappears and one actor twirls the slitted umbrella in front of the light, causing a strobe effect, while the others set up stacked chairs for Humpty-Dumpty to sit on. The Queen, hunched over with the shawl around her head like an old woman, has turned into the Sheep. The Forest has opened its umbrellas and turned them into the walls of the Sheep's Shop.)* What is it you want to buy?

ALICE: *(Who has fallen dizzily to the ground after being twirled around by the Queen.)* To buy?

LARRY: Buy me. *(He and Gerry grab Queen's shawl and begin to wave it up and down.)*

ALICE: I don't know right now. I should like to look all about me if I may.

SHEEP: You can look in front of you and on both sides but you can't look all around you unless you have eyes in the back of your head.

ALICE: *(Jerry has thrown an egg into the bouncing shawl.)* Things float about here so.

SHEEP: Now what is it you want to buy? Make up your mind.

ALICE: I'll take that egg.

SHEEP: Oh, I never put things into people's hands; that will never do. They have to get it for themselves. *(She grabs the egg from the shawl. The men use the shawl to conceal the Queen from Alice. When she runs out from behind the shawl Alice follows and the men cover Jerry with it. Jerry has climbed up and has seated himself on the stack of chairs. All the actors except the one playing Humpty play a keep-away game with the egg. Alice runs to each but they throw the egg to someone else just before she gets to them.)*

SASKIA: Get it for yourself.

GERRY: Get it for yourself.

LARRY: I never put things into people's hands.

TOM: Would you excuse me? *(All except Alice huddle together, concealing the egg from her. As she goes to each they open their cupped hands, revealing that they do not have the egg. When she finally gets to Tom, the last, she is totally confused.)* Get it for yourself. Get it for yourself.

LARRY: Psssssst. *(Pointing to the veiled Humpty.)*

ALICE: *(As she rips the shawl off of Humpty.)* How exactly like an egg he is. *(During the Humpty scene, the other actors hold Humpty up by pulling on imaginary ropes.)*

Sometimes I have believed in as many as six impossible things before breakfast.

What is it you want to buy?

HUMPTY: It's very annoying being called an egg.

TOM: *(Whispers to Alice.)* Watch out for the rope.

ALICE: I said you *looked* like an egg . . . some eggs are very handsome, you know. . . .

HUMPTY: *(Holding up an egg to show her. Pause.)* . . . State your name and business.

ALICE: My name is Alice. . . .

HUMPTY: That's a silly enough name . . . what does it mean?

ALICE: Must a name mean something?

HUMPTY: Of course; my name means the shape I am. And a good good handsome shape it is too. With a name like yours, you could be any shape, almost. *(He totters on the stack of chairs.)*

ALICE: Why do you sit up there all by yourself?

HUMPTY: Because there's nobody with me. Did you think I couldn't answer that? Go on, ask me another.

ALICE: No . . . don't you think you'd be safer here on the ground?

HUMPTY: What easy riddles you ask. No, I don't think I'd be safer there on the ground . . . you see, even if I were to . . . well, you know . . . of course, there's no chance, no chance whatsoever, but let us suppose I were to . . . FALL. *(Makes sudden, violent gesture which causes chairs to rock.)*

ALICE: Don't do that.

HUMPTY: Well, y'see, the White King has promised me that . . . he'd send all of his horses and all . . .

ALICE: *(Speaking with him.)* . . . And all of his men . . . yeah.

HUMPTY: Oh, yeah . . . you've been eavesdropping as well . . . listening at the doors . . . and down chimneys . . . you couldn't have known that . . . it was . . .

ALICE: . . . But I read it in a book.

HUMPTY: You read it . . . in a book? Oh, yes. They could put something like that in a book. Call it a history of England . . . take a good look at me, my dear . . . I am one who has spoken with a king. Mayhap you shall never see such another . . . oh, but I'm not proud. Here. You can shake my hand. *(She does so.)* Now, I have a question for you . . . how old did you say you were?

ALICE: Seven and a half.

Things float about here so.

HUMPTY: Wrong. You didn't say a word like that . . . seven and a half, hmmmm? . . . Seven years and six months, I suppose . . . that's a very uncomfortable sort of an age . . . if you'd asked my advice I'd have said, "Leave off at seven." . . . Of course, it's too late for that now.

ALICE: One can't help growing older.

HUMPTY: Ahh. One can't perhaps, but two always can. With a little bit of help you could have left off bang, right at seven. Now there's glory for you.

ALICE: "Glory"?

HUMPTY: I mean, there's a nice knock-down argument for you.

ALICE: Glory doesn't mean a nice knock-down argument.

HUMPTY: *(Imitating Nixon.)* May I make one thing perfectly clear . . . when I use a word it means precisely what I choose it to mean. Nothing more and nothing less.

ALICE: The question is whether you can make words mean so many different things.

HUMPTY: No, the question is, which is to be master, and that's all. IMPENETRABILITY. That's what I always say.

ALICE: But what do you mean by impenetrability?

HUMPTY: Ahh, by "impenetrability" I meant: we've-had-about-enough-of-this-subject-and-since-I-don't-suppose-you-mean-to-stop-here-all-the-rest-of-your-life-why-don't-you-tell-me-what-you-mean-to-do-next.

ALICE: That's an awful lot for one word to mean.

HUMPTY: When I work a word extra, I pay it extra.

ALICE: You're very clever with words. No, really. You even remind me a little of my friend . . . he recites poetry to me.

HUMPTY: I can recite poetry as well as the next fellow when it comes to that.

ALICE: Oh, it needn't come to that.

HUMPTY: This poem that I was going to recite was written entirely for your benefit.

ALICE: Ohhhh, . . . thank you. *(He motions for her to sit, she does so.)*

HUMPTY: In winter when the fields are white I sing this song for your delight . . . only I don't sing it . . . well, you know. . . .

ALICE: I can see that you don't.

HUMPTY: . . . In spring when woods are getting green, I'll try and tell you what I mean.

ALICE: Thank you.

HUMPTY: In summer when the days are long, perhaps you'll understand the song. In autumn when the leaves are brown, take pen and ink and write it down. . . .

ALICE: I will . . . but I don't know if I'll remember it that long, I have . . .

HUMPTY: You know, you needn't go on making remarks like that; I sent a message to the fish, I told them, "This is what I wish." But the little fishes of the sea, they sent an answer back to me. The little fishes' answer was, "We cannot do it Sir, because . . ."

ALICE: Excuse me, I don't understand what you wanted the fishes to . . .

HUMPTY: It gets easier further on! I sent to them again to say, "It would be better to obey." But the little fishes answered, with that grin, "Why, what a temper you are in." I told them once; I told them twice; they wouldn't listen to advice. So I took the corkscrew from the shelf, and I went to do this deed myself. And when I found that the door was locked, I pushed and pulled, I kicked and knocked. When I found that the door was shut, I . . . tried to turn the handle, buuuuuttttt . . . (He curls himself up into a ball with his face buried in his arms and the egg pressed against his face.)

Goodbye?

ALICE: Is that all?

HUMPTY: That's all. Goodbye.

ALICE: Goodbye? . . . (She gets up and gently taps Humpty.) . . . Till we meet again?

HUMPTY: I should not know you if we did meet again . . . you're so exactly like all of the others.

ALICE: It's my face that one goes by, generally.

HUMPTY: That's just what I was referring to: your face. It's so exactly like everyone else's . . . I mean . . . there it is, with the nose in the middle, and eyes on either side of the nose, and a mouth down below . . . now . . . if you had, say, that eye . . . over there . . . or the mouth . . . up there . . .

ALICE: That wouldn't look nice.

HUMPTY: Wait until you've tried.

ALICE: Goodbye. (She turns to go and freezes.)

HUMPTY: Goodbye? . . . (Pause. He smashes the egg against his head and hurls *himself to the ground. Alice turns and freezes in horrified position as all the other actors, except for one playing the White Knight, form a funeral procession and carry Humpty's rigid body off stage. Alice follows procession but is left standing alone. The White Knight, who has been hiding behind the table, sneaks up on Alice, spins her around and grabs her by the throat. She hits him in the head and knocks him to the floor.)*

WHITE KNIGHT: It was a glorious victory, wasn't it?

ALICE: I don't know. I don't want to be anybody's prisoner; I want to be a Queen.

WHITE KNIGHT: *(Getting up and walking stiffly towards her.)* So you shall, as soon as you've crossed the next brook, and I'll take you as far as the end of the wood, but then I must come back. That's the end of my move. *(He hits his head.)* Clang! Clang!

ALICE: You need help.

WHITE KNIGHT: *(Indistinct mumbling; "Help me off with my helmet," as if his speech were muffled.)* Clang. Clang. Clang. *(He bends over from the waist.)* Creeeeeak. *(Muffled speech.)*

ALICE: What . . . what . . . oh, your helmet. *(She puts her arms around his head and pretends to pull.)* I've got it . . . *(He flips her over his shoulder. She springs to her feet as he comes crashing down almost on top of her. Alice takes karate stance.)* Okay. Come on.

WHITE KNIGHT: *(Suddenly going from his karate stance to stretching his arms out in front of him.)* I see you're admiring my little box. That's to keep clothes and sandwiches in. I keep it upside-down, so that the rain can't get in. It's an invention of my own. You may try it if you like.

ALICE: But if you keep it upside-down, everything can fall out.

WHITE KNIGHT: Everything has fallen out and the box is no good without them. *(He places the imaginary box down.)* Can you guess why I did that? Because it's best to be prepared for everything. That's why my horse has those anklets 'round his feet. *(He points.)*

ALICE: What are they for?

WHITE KNIGHT: To guard against the bites of sharks. *(She tries to leave but he turns himself into a shark, grabs her around the ankle and bites her leg. Alice slaps him and he lets go.)* I'd better go. Help me on my horse and I'll be on my way. *(Alice shakes her head.)* Help me on my horse.

ALICE: No, No, No.

WHITE KNIGHT: Help me on my horse. *(He comes menacingly towards her and*

It was a glorious victory, wasn't it?

she immediately cups her hands to help him up on his imaginary horse.) It's over there. *(She moves to where he points. He begins to mount but stops abruptly.)* Is your hair well fastened on?

ALICE: In the usual fashion.

WHITE KNIGHT: Oh, that's not nearly enough. The wind around here is as strong as soup. But I have a plan for keeping it from falling off. Would you like to hear it? *(Alice nods and he grabs her hair and demonstrates as he speaks.)* First you take an upright stick, and then you make your hair creep up it like a fruit tree. Now the only . . . problem with hair is that it hangs downward, you know. Nothing ever falls upwards, you see what I mean? It's an invention of my own. You may try it if you like.

ALICE: It's not very comfortable.

WHITE KNIGHT: Do you know what the great art of riding is? It's just to keep your balance. Like this. *(He jumps onto her back.)* Giddy-up. *(Alice falls and they both land on the ground with Alice on top.)* Aaaaaaaaaah.

ALICE: This is ridiculous. Maybe you ought to get yourself a little wooden horse. You know, the kind with the wheels.

WHITE KNIGHT: Does that kind go more smoothly?

ALICE: It's better than a live one.

WHITE KNIGHT: Well, maybe I'll get myself one . . . or two . . . I'll get several. Why not?

ALICE: Why not?

WHITE KNIGHT: Because I'm a great hand at inventing things. I daresay you noticed the last time you helped me up, I was looking rather thoughtful. . . .

ALICE: You were great.

WHITE KNIGHT: Well, just then I was thinking of a new way of getting over a gate. Would you like to hear it?

ALICE: No. No, I said I didn't want to hear it. *(He goes on.)* I'm not listening.

WHITE KNIGHT: I'll tell you how I came to think of it. You see, I said to myself, "The only problem is with the feet; the head is high enough already," if you know what I mean. Here, help. *(He scoops her up and lays her down on the ground in front of him.)* Gate.

ALICE: No. No, leave me out of this.

WHITE KNIGHT: Now, first I put my head on top of the gate, like this, you see?

Everything has fallen out . . .

To guard against the bites of sharks.

Do you know what the great art of riding is?

(*He demonstrates, using her as the gate.*) Then I stand on my head, like this. Then I'm over, you see?

ALICE: That's going to be a little hard to do.

WHITE KNIGHT: I don't know . . . I haven't tried it on a real gate yet so I can't say for certain, YET.

ALICE: No, I think it's impossible.

WHITE KNIGHT: It is not impossible. (*He rests his head on her knees, she reaches for him but he suddenly looks up at her and grabs something off her head.*) Aaaaahhhhh!

ALICE: What?

WHITE KNIGHT: (*Taking the imaginary object and placing it on his own head, he strikes at it.*) Clang. Clang.

ALICE: (*Taking his head in her hands.*) Oh, what a beautiful helmet. Is that an invention of your own?

WHITE KNIGHT: Yes, but I've invented a better one than that. It was shaped like a sugar-loaf. So whenever I fell off my horse, it hit the ground right away and I didn't have very far to fall. Like this, you see? (*He falls with a rigid body to the floor.*) But there was the danger of falling into it, to be sure. (*Alice runs over to him and tries to silence him by putting her hands over his mouth, but he pushes her away and continues.*) I did that once, and the worst part of that was that the other White Knight came along and he put it on because he thought it was his own helmet, do you know what I mean? It took hours and hours to get me out. I was stuck fast as . . . as lightning, do you know what I mean?

ALICE: No, that's a different kind of fastness.

WHITE KNIGHT: It was all kinds of fastness with me, I can assure you. But it was careless of him to put another man's helmet on . . . and with the man in it, too.

ALICE: Please. How can you go on talking like that?

WHITE KNIGHT: What difference does it make whether I go on talking? My mind . . . my mind keeps on inventing new things. Now the cleverest thing of the sort that I ever invented was a new pudding during the meat course. (*Pause.*) You say, "In time for the next course?"

ALICE: No, please. I know.

WHITE KNIGHT: Then say it. (*Grabbing her.*) Say IT!

ALICE: In time for the next course.

WHITE KNIGHT: Of course not. (*Laughs at his own joke.*) In time for the next

Then I stand on my head, like this.

Then I'm over, you see?

It is not impossible.

course? Of COURSE not. In fact, I don't think that pudding ever was cooked. I don't think that pudding ever will be cooked. And yet, it was a very clever pudding to invent.

ALICE: What did you mean it to be made out of?

WHITE KNIGHT: Blotting paper.

ALICE: No, that doesn't sound very nice.

WHITE KNIGHT: Not very nice by itself, perhaps. But you have no idea what a difference it makes when you mix it with other things . . . like gunpowder and sealing wax. *(He stirs a big imaginary pot and creates an explosion.)* Barroom.

ALICE: *(Covering her ears.)* No, no more. Please.

WHITE KNIGHT: I've got to go. But you look a little sad. Let me sing you a little song first to comfort you and then I'll be on my way.

ALICE: Is it long?

WHITE KNIGHT: Yes, it's long, but it's very beautiful. Everybody who hears me sing it, either it brings tears to their eyes or else. . . .

ALICE: Or else what?

WHITE KNIGHT: Or else it doesn't, and you know. *(He kneels beside her.)* Now, the name of the song is called "Haddock's Eyes."

ALICE: Oh, that's the name of the song, is it?

WHITE KNIGHT: No, you don't understand . . . that's what the name is called. The name really is "The Aged, Aged Man."

ALICE: Then I should have said, "That's what the song is called."

WHITE KNIGHT: No, you shouldn't; that's quite another thing. The song is called "Ways and Means." But that's only what it's called, you know.

ALICE: What is the song.

WHITE KNIGHT: I was just coming to that. The song really is "A-Sitting on a Gate" and the tune's my own invention: *(Sings song in the style of Bob Dylan.)*

I'll tell thee everything I can, there's little to relate,
I saw an aged, aged man, a-sitting on a gate.
"Who are you, aged man?" I said, "And how is it you live?" And his answer
   trickled through my head, like water through a sieve.
He said, "I look for butterflies that sleep among the wheat.
I make them into mutton pies, and sell them in the street.
I sell them unto men," he said, "who sail on stormy seas.

In time for the next course? Of COURSE not.

And that's the way I get my bread—a trifle, if you please."
But I was thinking of a plan to dye one's whiskers green,
And always use so large a fan, that they could not be seen.
So having no reply to give to what the old man said,
"Come, tell me how you live," I cried, and thumped him on the head.

(He thumps Alice on the head by placing one hand on top of her head and hitting his own hand. Alice begins to cry.)

ALICE: No, no more, please. *(When he continues she throws herself at him and collapses into his arms.)*

WHITE KNIGHT: He said, "I look for haddock's eyes among the heather bright,
And work them into waistcoat buttons in the silent night.
And these I do not sell for gold or coin of silvery shine,
But for a copper halfpenny and that will purchase nine.
I sometimes dig for buttered rolls," *(He breaks off here to get Alice's attention.)*
Hey! Dig for buttered rolls. *(He makes digging gestures. Alice begins to laugh so hard that the Knight has to silence her in order to continue. Her laughter turns into sobs as the poem progresses.)*

No, no more, please.

"Or set limed twigs for crabs.
I sometimes search the grassy knolls for wheels of hansom cabs,
And that's the way"—he gave a wink—"by which I get my wealth,
And very gladly will I drink your honor's noble health."
And now if e'er by chance I put my fingers into glue,
Or madly squeeze a right-hand foot into a left-hand shoe,
Or drop upon my toe a very heavy weight,
I weep, for it reminds me so of that old man I used to know—
Whose look was mild, whose speech was slow,
Whose hair was whiter than the snow,
Whose face was very like a crow,
With eyes like cinders, all aglow,
Who seemed distracted with his woe,
Who rocked his body to and fro,
And muttered mumblingly and low,
As if his mouth were full of dough,
Who snorted like a buffalo—
That summer evening long ago,
A-sitting on a gate.

(They pause a minute in silence in each other's arms and then the Knight pulls himself up and begins to exit.) You've only a few yards to go, down the hill and over that little brook, and then you'll be a queen. But first you'll stay and see me off? If you take out your handkerchief and wave it to me as I go around the bend in the road, I think it will encourage me, you know what I mean? Did you like the song?

I hunt for haddock's eyes among the heather bright!

(Alice nods, and then shakes her head violently and then begins to nod again totally confused.) I hope so. You didn't cry nearly so much as I thought you would. And it's the best song I know. I don't know any better songs than that. *(Exits mumbling.)* It's the best one in my repertoire.

ALICE: I liked the song. . . . *(Alone.)* . . . I liked the song . . . *(Half calling after him and half to herself.)* I liked the song. *(She falls back onto the ground as if falling back into a sleep. A short pause and then the first fall repeats itself, only this time it is done backwards. Alice is tossed from person to person as she was in the beginning but in reverse order.)*

ALL: Whiskers and ears my oh. Whiskers and ears my oh.

DODGSON: Over was fall the and leaves dry and sticks of bed a on came she down thump thump suddenly when eat cats do cats eat bats do bats eat cats do but. Know you mouse a like very that's and bat a catch might you but air the in mice no are there. Down, down, down, me with here down were you wish I dear my Dinah end an to come never fall the would. Down, down, down home at me think all they'll brave how down-stairs falling of nothing think I'll this as fall a such after well! *(All freeze, recreating the tableau of Alice going into the hole but this time when it comes to life again, she is coming out of it. As Dodgson resumes speaking the others begin to move again.)* It after went she down minute another in her by close ran eyes pink with rabbit white the suddenly when considering do to nothing and day hot the with tired rather getting bank the on sitting sister her and . . . *(Alice falls back into her sister's lap, small intake of breath.)* Alice! *(The reverse fall ends, momentary tableau.)*

Blackout.

I liked the song . . . I liked the song.

Over was fall . . .

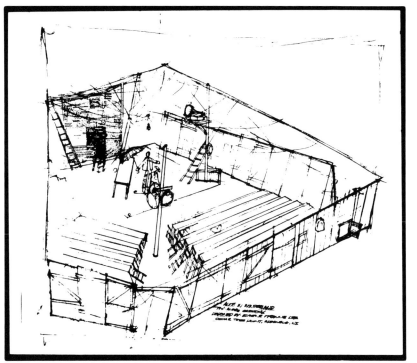

Sketch of original set by Eugene Lee

After seeing one rehearsal
of Alice and talking to Andre, I knew
the costumes had to be
quilted and that they had to resemble what
the actors wore while they were working.
Larry's pants were made from old
packing blankets, Gerry Bamman's overalls
from a comforter. I found a fencing
costume for Saskia and made her
skirt out of a lot of old petticoats.
Jerry Mayer's pants came from
an old quilt I had and Tommy's costume
from one I found. Angela's
was the last costume to be finished.
It was originally a robe
that I made into a jumper and
the sleeves are parts of
old petticoats.
　　　　　　　. . . Franne Lee

The
Plastiques

DETAILS OF AN EXERCISE
ORIGINALLY DEVELOPED BY JERZY GROTOWSKI
AND THE POLISH LABORATORY THEATER

**GERRY
BAMMAN**

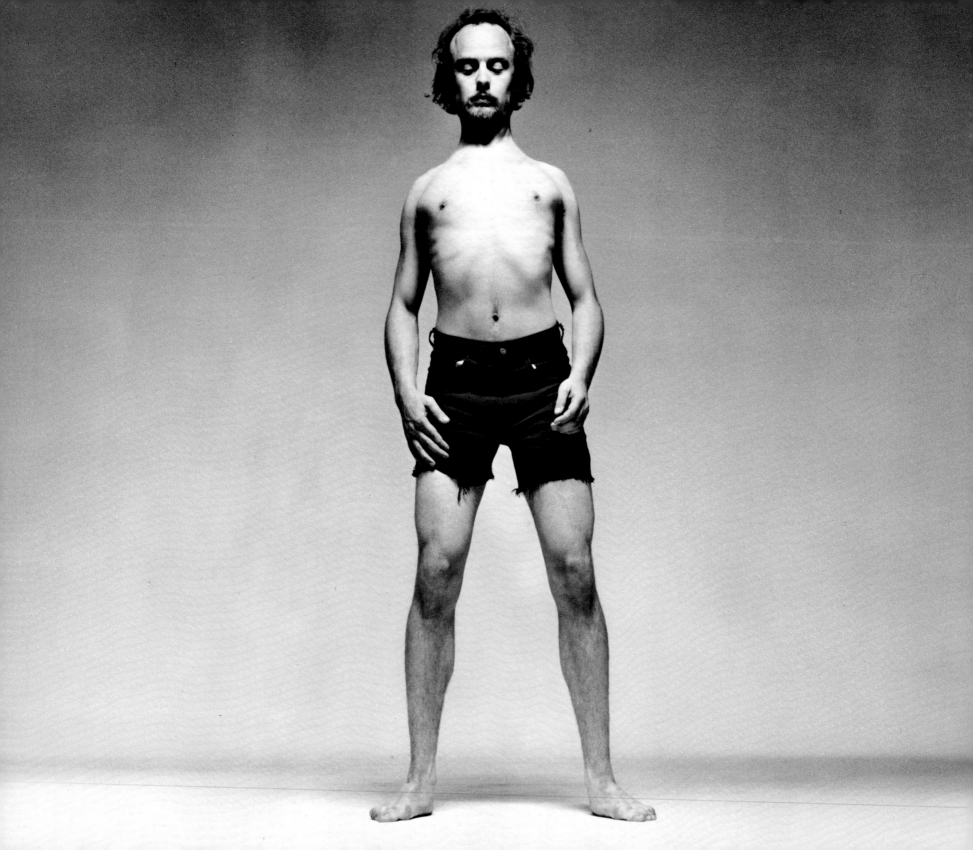

The text for this book
was set in Helvetica Light by the Plimpton Corporation.

———————————

This book was printed in
the Stonetone process by Rapoport Printing Corporation
on 80 pound Wedgewood dull coated stock
supplied from Champion Papers, Inc.
and bound by Sendor Bindery.